COMING OF
AGE IN ACADEME

Coming of Age in Academe

JANE ROLAND MARTIN

*With a foreword
by Gloria Steinem*

REKINDLING
WOMEN'S
HOPES
AND
REFORMING
THE
ACADEMY

Routledge
New York and London

Published in 2000 by
Routledge
29 West 35th Street
New York, NY 10001

Published in Great Britain by
Routledge
11 New Fetter Lane
London EC4P 4EE

Library of Congress Cataloging-in-Publication Data

Martin, Jane Roland, 1929–
      Coming of age in academe: rekindling women's hopes and reforming
   the academy / by Jane Roland Martin.
            p.   cm.
      Includes bibliographical references and index.
      ISBN 0–415–92487–1 (hard). —ISBN 0–415–92488-X (pbk).
      1. Feminism and education—United States. 2. Women—Education (Higher)—
United States. 3. Universities and colleges—United States—Sociological aspects. 4.
Educational change—United States. I. Title.
LC197.M37   1999
379.1'9822—dc21   99-20656
                                                                            CIP

To Aimée
and Nina

CONTENTS

FOREWORD

by Gloria Steinem

On the average of several times a month for the past thirty years, I've given a lecture and held an organizing meeting at one of the 3,200 colleges and universities in this country.

Usually, this means I've been invited by students as one of the speakers brought by their activities' fees, often as a joint effort among the Women's Center, African-American, environmental, gay and lesbian, and other groups trying to balance speakers' programs that otherwise lean heavily toward newly diselected politicians and media stars.

In other words, I'm a free agent, with no worries about tenure, faculty politics, publishing in scholarly journals, or other hurdles in the obstacle course that must be run by academics. As an itinerant feminist organizer, my only job is to create a few hours of safe space for students, faculty, staff, and people from the community, give a speech so they have something shared to respond to, and invite a brainstorming session on how to change whatever they think needs changing. The goal is not only to create more fairness in this place of learning, teaching, and living, but to practice activism for the larger world.

In this way, I've witnessed from the outside the same three decades that veteran academic Jane Roland Martin is writing about after thirty years as a professor on the inside. I can vouch for the validity of her thesis that academic acceptance too often demands the rejection of authenticity—one's own, other people's, and sometimes of whole chunks of human experience. As she says:

> I came to see that the academy charges an exorbitant admission fee to those women who wish to belong. But that is the least of it. In turning male and female members alike away from the lived experience of real people in the real world, and especially from society's desperately urgent problems, the academy creates a brain drain within the culture at large.

She is addressing not only the traditional isolation of the ivory tower, but also its current skill at entrapping the very groups that once set out to liberate it. Both of us are trying to bridge, as she puts it wryly, "the great gulf between those who search for knowledge and those who wish to improve society."

If this ambitious book succeeds, workers inside the academy will feel supported in confronting such occupational hazards as retreating into history or theory (instead of also putting those lessons to current use), distancing from social problems and politics (instead of seeing the campus as a source of solutions and votes as well as learning), and creating a closed circle that speaks a language no one else can understand (instead of striving for clarity and influence beyond academia). People outside will be encouraged to treat the academy as a source of continuing wisdom, not a one-time event in our lives or a separate universe.

I salute Martin's courage in making waves as one of the hardy band of academic activists who are resisting insularity, not to mention fighting the budget-cutting war against public universities, and efforts to turn back women's studies, African-American studies, Asian-American studies, gay and lesbian studies; all the newer areas of scholarship that should be called "remedial studies" to indicate that the establishment is in need of remediation.

Perhaps her energy is partly due to the fact that almost all of her teaching years were spent at the University of Massachusetts, rather than, say, Harvard, where she taught briefly. It's been my experience that the more elitist the institution, the less open it is to outsiders, if only because competition among the powerful is so intense that the less powerful get less space. In the proportion of tenured faculty who are females of any race, for example, Harvard ranks at the very bottom of the nation, with males occupying seven out of eight tenured positions, and an average of one woman hired for every 250 positions filled over the past twenty-four years. It also came late to African-American studies (only student riots in the 1960s, plus a big-time endowment raised by faculty, brought Harvard to the status it now enjoys), little to women's studies, and reluctantly to all the other areas of "remedial studies."

On the other hand, because I've spent more time at community colleges, women's colleges, colleges that are historically African American, and universities far from the Ivy League, I'm more cheerful than she is. With little motive to preserve the status quo, those campuses are less likely to shroud knowledge in esoteric language, reward the aerialized view, invent labels that have little relevance outside academia, and otherwise perpetuate the practices she is exposing. Yet those institutions contribute to the national trend documented by the American Association of University Professors over the past twenty years: the number of tenured males is increasing 30 percent faster than that of tenured females. Many women academics are also kept in part-time or temporary positions, overworked, underpaid, and without the freedom to express themselves that comes with tenure. It's a kind of negative action that has gotten lost in the furor over affirmative action. At four-year colleges in general, the result is clear: most male faculty are tenured; most female faculty are not.

I share Martin's worry that the academy (meaning all of higher learning) is gradually co-opting women and new areas of scholarship by and about the female half of the world—as well as men whose wisdom comes from the margins, and remedial studies in general—more than vice versa. I would go a step further and add that, despite inspiring exceptions, the academy is tougher to change than business. There, popularity with consumers creates a bottom line, an objective measure of competence, which provides a way around the hierarchy. In academia, however, good teachers who are beloved by their students regularly fail to receive tenure or promotion, and even lose jobs, because they are not published in refereed journals, or approved by departmental colleagues; the very gatekeepers whose authority they may be challenging.

Perhaps the main thing that academia shares with business is a far greater acceptance of new groups of students than new groups of faculty; that is, consumers who pay rather than employees who get paid. As for the famous glass ceiling in corporations, this exists on campuses, too, but faculty women can't strike out on their own as entrepreneurs—something women in business are doing at three times the rate of men. There is no equivalent freedom in academia.

Nonetheless, Martin makes clear that she is only criticizing what she loves. She sees the academy as an area where students should be able to examine their own and others' experience, not feel estranged from it; a birthplace of innovation and activism, not caution and wasteful competition; a thinktank for theory that informs practice—and vice versa—not one that elevates theorizing as an end in itself.

It helps that, as a philosopher of education, Martin has spent her professional life in two very different areas: philosophy, which tends to be taken seriously because it is theoretical and mostly male, and education, which tends to be taken less seriously because it is practical and mostly female. This double vision has given her an imagination of what a truly equal-opportunity academy might look like, and fueled her anger that it is still so far from the reality.

Having a foot in both camps also allows her to explain why academia is deprived, not only of women's full participation as what she calls the "co-professoriate of the future," but also of whole areas that have been wrongly devalued because of their identification with females. I would add to this list the study of childrearing, from ancient indigenous methods that seem to have created the most self-respecting and least violent people, to a wide-and-deep understanding of family structures. Certainly, our earliest training is the root of all political systems: hierarchical families and authoritarian childrearing methods create authoritarian societies (and vice versa); democratic families and child-respecting methods give self-authority and democracy their start. Yet where are the political science courses that begin with forms of family and childrearing?

One disheartening result is that women in academia sometimes have to disqualify crucial parts of their own lived histories, and become estranged from their mothers, grandmothers, even from 1970s feminist scholars who grounded their pioneering scholarship in lived experience. Martin is most pained by the turn of some women's studies scholars away from critiques of society that contribute to action, and toward theory and critiques of each other's theories; by a conformity to educational mores where once there was a will to transform them; and by the coating of all this in an arcane language that only insiders understand.

Because Martin doesn't list any of the unhappy examples of this academic lingo, let me give you some of my favorite recurring phrases: *the poststructuralist marginalization of the reproduction of women's agency, decentering of the humanist subject consequent upon the postmodernist critique of subjectivity, discoursive formations as coherent bodies in which power relations and knowledge inhere.*

Even conversations may be studded with verbal tics that are as superfluous as a Valley Girl's use of "like," "for sure," and "way cool." However, unlike those, the academic versions seem designed to exclude. For example: "essentialist," "valorizing," "privileging," "counter-hegemonic," "hermeneutical," "deconstructionist," and "discourse" (which turns out to mean conversation). Perhaps there should be signs on every highway leading to Yale, Harvard, and so on: "Beware, Deconstruction Ahead."

Unlike feminist activists, journalists, and lovers of language who have also complained about academic obscurity, Martin cannot be accused of antiintellectualism. On the contrary, she is making an intellectual plea: words are meant to communicate, not cover up. Theory that isn't understandable will be left on the page. Even if occult language must be used to gain publication and tenure, to have the pleasure of rarified conversation, or to create the academic version of a gang, Martin still makes a great point: physicians have good reason to use specialized words, yet we ask them to explain in terms we can understand, and to empower us to make our own decisions. Whether we are academics, or those who desperately need academia's research and wisdom, why should we settle for anything less?

Fortunately, Martin sets a good example. You know she is very smart because you can understand every word she writes.

Take her explanation of the current academic use of *essentialism*, a catch-all word with little relevance off campus. Martin explains that this label got started as an understandable criticism of generalities based only on white women's experience. But then spread like a kudzu vine.

What it *should* mean can be seen from *essence*, which is defined in the *Oxford English Dictionary* as: "The totality of the properties, constituent elements, etc., without which it would cease to be the same thing; the indispensable and necessary attributes of a thing as opposed to those which it may have or not . . . "

This accurately describes biological determinism—that perpetual adversary of women's full humanity—including the argument of conservative suffragists (as opposed to feminist abolitionists) that females were intrinsically more moral, and less sexual than males. But whether used mostly by men for anti-equality purposes, as in the first case, or mostly by women for pro-equality ones, as in the second, essentialism connotes changelessness, immutability.

The current sloppy use of "essentialism" began when it was used to criticize generalizations about women's experience that failed to include such relevant differences as race, class, and sexuality; certainly a worthy cause. But it was so successful as a drop-dead charge that it was soon being used against almost any challenging statement about an experience of females, no matter how clearly grounded in culture, rather than biology; no matter how carefully qualified as a statement about some but not all females; and no matter how well documented. At the extreme, even using the category "women" has brought "essentialist" cries. (By the lights of some postmodernists and deconstructionists, everything is mutable, no two people experience the same thing; thus, there are no general statements. If you're curious about all this—or are facing such arguments—read *Nothing Mat(t)ers: A Feminist Critique of Postmodernism* by Somer Brodribb.[1]) Since shared experience is the basis for shared action, essentialism usually serves as a kind of nihilism that cuts off action at the pass by preventing any sense of connection.

In the sometimes cutthroat atmosphere of academia, places at the table are too few, and rewards for disqualifying female scholars or female-supporting theory (which often threatens the establishment by citing patterns of shared experience and discrimination) are obvious. *A Glossary of Feminist Theory*[2] puts it simply: "In contemporary feminist theory, if the charge of essentialism can be made to stick, the offending theory is sunk."

I've also noticed that this charge finds fertile ground among young women students who haven't yet experienced or admitted discrimination, don't want to believe they have to, and thus are open to dismissing any such suggestion on grounds that is "essentialist." On the other hand, bell hooks, a fearless academic whose writing remains rooted in experience, says she is often accused of being an essentialist when she cites her experience as a woman, but not when she cites her experience as an African American.

This highly selective use is a dead giveaway to a deeper priority: disqualifying the self-willed grouping of females, not necessarily groupings that include men, and not essentialist statements made by men about women. Thus, male academics and writers who really *are* biological determinists seem to be pretty much exempt. So do generalizations about "the Jewish experience," even though they paper over differences between Ashkenazi and Ethiopian, male and female, rich and poor. Discussions of, say, "Latin culture" don't seem to be called essentialist by the same academics who use it against Carol Gilligan's *In A Different Voice*. Nor would she have been as likely to be so labelled if the "voice" in question had been, say, working class.

In fact, Gilligan explained in the introduction to her 1982 work that she was documenting a culturally created experience, not an immutable one. As she wrote, "The different voice I describe . . . is not absolute, and the contrast between male and female voices are presented here to highlight a distinction between two modes of thought . . . rather than to represent a generalization about either sex."[3] Many readers outside academia recognized their own lived experience in her research, and made her book a rare crossover success. Within academia, Gilligan's challenges to Lawrence Kohlberg's famous six stages of moral development—derived from studying white boys and men only—revolutionized the field of ethics. Thus, those who wrongly categorize Gilligan as an essentialist are disqualifying one of the few scholars who successfully introduced new feminist ideas into the mainstream. One wonders if these two events are not connected. After all, academia suspects the popular. And even feminists may punish the strong member of their group—just as men tend to punish the weak member—as an unconscious way of policing gender roles.

This highly selective use of a negative label is far from unique. Take the case of "identity politics," a phrase that wasn't (and isn't) used against white Protestant males, though they've been gathering together on an exclusive basis for centuries. They often defend their academic turf and identity politics as synonymous with "Western civilization" or "excellence"—and get away with it. But gatherings of men and women of color, women of various races, gays and lesbians, and other challengers of the status quo, anyone who comes together for purposes of visibility and fairness, do find themselves so accused.

So don't be surprised if "essentialism," having been honed as a weapon against scholarship that might lead to connection and action among groups of women, is used against African-American studies, and other categories that also include men—but the wrong men. By 1997, Gloria Bird, a Native American, could write, "In academia, if one argues for any type of distinction, or uses any means to determine who is Indian, the argument is often dismissed as 'essentialist' . . . "[4] The plot thins.

❯ ❯ ❯

In my years of speaking on campus, I've come to trust the ability of audiences to cross any academic distance, and become an all-five-senses community. I look forward to that moment when someone on one side of the hall asks a question, someone on the other side answers it, and the group suddenly understands that neither I nor any other outsider was necessary in the first place. All the energy, expertise, and activist ideas were present all along.

That's also the message of this book. Jane Roland Martin brings us together to think about the energy being wasted on an old game, and the possibilities if those energies were set free.

Then it's up to us.

ACKNOWLEDGMENTS

The Society of Feminist Scholars and Their Friends is a fig-
ment of the author's imagination. The June 1991 conference at
the University of Calgary where the material on essentialism in
Part One of this book was initially presented was very real,
however, and I am grateful to Maggie Osler for inviting me to
participate in it. I am grateful, too, to the editors of *Signs* for
publishing a version of the paper I read on that occasion,
"Methodological Essentialism, False Difference, and Other
Dangerous Traps,"[1] and my sequel to it, "Aerial Distance, Esotericism, and Other Closely Related Traps,"[2] I also wish to
thank the many audiences in Norway and Sweden with whom
I discussed my research on essentialism, aerial distance, and
esotericism during the fall of 1995, as well as the graduate students at Lund University who invited me to present my work
on aerial distance at their June 1996 conference, Feminist Per-
spectives on International Relations.

The organizing concept of Part Two of this volume was first
presented at the February 1996 conference, Gender and the
Higher Education Classroom, held at Duke University. I am
grateful to the law students who invited me to give the keynote
address at that event and then published a revised version of

Acknowledgments

"Bound for the Promised Land: The Gendered Character of Higher Education" in the *Duke Journal of Gender Law & Policy*.[3] My thanks also to Else-Marie Staberg for arranging a guest professorship for me at the Centre for Women's Studies at the University of Umeå in May 1997; to Inga Elgqvist-Saltzman and Christina Florin for inviting me to deliver the opening address at an August 1997 conference in Stockholm on Women and Higher Education; and to the organizing committee of the August 1998 European Conference on Gender Equality in Higher Education in Helsinki for asking me to speak at the opening ceremony. In addition to being encouraged on all three occasions to present my immigrant interpretation of women's experience in the academy, I had the rare privilege of being able to discuss the problems I deal with in this book to my heart's content with scholars from different countries and in a range of disciplines. At the Stockholm conference I quite unexpectedly had the good fortune also to be invited to test out on my audience a number of the ideas I include in Part Three of this volume.

As ever, I am indebted to Ann Diller, Susan Franzosa, Barbara Houston, Michael Martin, Beebe Nelson, Jennifer Radden, and Janet Farrell Smith for their comments and constructive criticisms of early drafts of various sections of this book, and to Michael Martin for reading the final draft of the whole thing. In addition, I wish to thank Patricia Mann for her very helpful critical reading of an early version of the entire manuscript; an anonymous publisher's reader whose advice about voice, audience, and my own positioning of myself improved this book immeasurably; Jean O'Barr for reading an early and late version of the book and making invaluable suggestions; Hilde Hein for discussing several key ideas in the book with me; the students in the seminar on gender and higher education I offered in the fall of 1996 at the Harvard

Graduate School of Education for teaching me so much about my topic; Mary Woods for giving me the right words; and Gloria Steinem for so generously agreeing to write the Foreword to this book. Finally, I want to thank Heidi Freund, publishing director at Routledge, for her boundless enthusiasm and faith in this project, and Jennifer Hirshlag, production editor, for her fine editorial eye and skills.

PREFACE

When Margaret Mead went to Samoa she chose to concentrate on adolescent girls because, as a woman, she could hope to achieve greater intimacy working with girls rather than with boys.[1] When in my imagination I made three expeditions across the academy's terrain, I chose to study the practices of feminist scholars for much the same reason. As a feminist scholar myself, this was the group I had the greatest access to; these were the people I knew best. Just as Mead decided to focus her fieldwork on adolescents rather than on adult women because knowledge of their joys and difficulties was relatively slight, I focused mine on feminist scholars rather than the other women of academe because so little was known about the problems we face and the challenges we confront.

Mead knew that to understand the adolescent girls it was necessary to grasp "the whole social life of Samoa."[2] On my expeditions I soon learned that to comprehend the practices of feminist scholars it is imperative to understand the academy's mores. And here is where she and I part company. Writing as an anthropologist, Mead saw her task to be that of giving as lucid a description of Samoan culture as she could. Cultural critique was not her business. Critical analysis is a philosopher's bread and butter, however, and a philosopher is what I am. In coming to understand the academy's mores, I came to see that the academy charges an exorbitant admission fee to those women who wish to belong. But that is the least of it. In turning male and female members alike away from the lived experience of real people in the real world, and especially from society's desperately urgent problems, the academy creates a "brain drain" within the culture at large.

Mead was twenty-three and at the beginning of her career when she arrived in Samoa. When I set out on my first expedition I was approaching the end of mine. Her goal in writing *Coming of Age in Samoa* was to communicate with teachers and parents—the people who had most to do with adolescents. The object of this book is to communicate with women and men both in and outside the academy who care deeply about the nature of higher education, about the education of women, about gender equality, and about the great gulf between those who search for knowledge and those who wish to improve society.

I also write for everyone who cares about the future of feminism, womanism, women's liberation—whatever one's phrase for empowerment and freedom—and especially for my sister scholars and our daughters at a time when we are an embattled group. I do so as a feminist scholar and philosopher who spent years inside the academy teaching philosophy and women's studies and doing research in both, and I do so in a constructive spirit. I leave it to others to trivialize and satirize feminist scholarship, to belittle and chastise the scholars for looking at the world as if all women mattered. The wholesale condemnation of feminist research and scholarship has become a kind of national pastime in the United States, and I want no part of it. Although I scrutinize what feminist scholars have said about their own inquiries and question here some of the academic mores that they appear to have made their own, I write as an advocate of diverse and inclusive feminist theory and research, not a foe. Just as Mead became a partisan of the adolescents she studied, I wish to stand up and be counted as one who applauds the successes of feminist scholarship, believes firmly in its still-to-be-realized possibilities, and devoutly hopes that it will continue to fulfill its enormous potential.

I also want to be counted as one who considers the academy an institution in need of reform. Mead said that the main lesson to be learned from the Samoan picture was that adolescence is not necessarily a time of stress and strain; cultural conditions make it so.[3] Right now, to be a feminist scholar in the academy is to experience stress and strain on a daily basis. Having gone into the field and observed my own kind from the perspective of an insider who always felt like an outsider and with the eyes of someone who has devoted most of her academic life to the philosophical study of education, I know that this need not be so. From the very start, Mead made it clear that her book about Samoa was mainly concerned with education.[4] This book is also about education. It is about the habits and customs of the academy, about the myriad ways in which they estrange both women and men from women, about the dangerous implications of these practices for men, women, and society, and about the reforms that need to be made.

What Price Women's Belonging?

INTRODUCTION

These are heady times for feminist scholars. In 1929 Virginia Woolf told university women, "it is necessary to have five hundred a year and a room with a lock on the door if you are to write fiction or poetry."[1] Today, women who analyze fiction and poetry, write treatises about knowledge and power, critique science and technology, and discuss gender from a feminist perspective have professorships and offices of their own. We also win grants, receive awards, occupy endowed chairs.

Sixty years after the publication of Woolf's *A Room of One's Own*, a feminist literary critic describes herself as "centrally in the academy."[2] Her colleague says that feminism is embedded "firmly in the academy."[3] One year later, a feminist philosopher cites the great change in the professional situation of academic feminists in the United States since 1980. Then we were outsiders, she says, and now we have been "accepted."[4] Two years later the Modern Language Association of America publishes a volume on the transformation of English and American literary studies containing an entire chapter on developments in feminist criticism and an affirmation by the editors that "virtually every field has been altered, sometimes radically, by the recovery of lost or marginalized texts of women writers."[5] Next, the feminist journal *Hypatia* prints a pair of articles announcing the "arrival" of feminist philosophy. And in 1996, the journal *Signs* publishes an article that begins, "To anyone working in the China Studies field it is apparent that, in the 1990s, 'women's studies' has become firmly established as a subfield of the discipline."[6]

How things have changed! In *Three Guineas* Woolf invited readers to stand on the bridge connecting two worlds—private and public, home and professions, women's and men's—and "fix our eyes upon the procession—the procession of sons of educated men."[7] There go our brothers, she said: "We have to ask ourselves, here and now, do we wish to join the procession, or don't we? On what terms shall we join the procession? Above all, where is it leading us, the procession of educated men?"[8] In 1938, the few women Woolf could see were traipsing along at the tail end of the procession. When I joined the procession in 1961, my Ph.D. in hand, there were more women in the procession. As I write, it is hard to find a woman who is not bound for the Promised Land.

Of the educated men—clearly white and European—in the procession across the bridge, Woolf remarked:

> They lose their senses. Sight goes. They have no time to look at pictures. Sound goes. They have no time to listen to music. Speech goes. They have no time for conversation. They lose their sense of proportion—the relations between one thing and another. Humanity goes. Money making becomes so important that they must work by night as well as by day. Health goes.[9]

The question she asked was: How can women be educated and enter the professions and yet remain "civilized human beings; human beings, that is, who wish to prevent war"?[10]

My question is: How can feminist scholars find acceptance in the academy without losing sight of their mothers, daughters, sisters, half-sisters, female cousins, and aunts—which means females of all classes, races, sexualities, and states of being?

Without cutting ourselves off from the sound of women's voices. Without forgetting how to speak to other women. Without severing ourselves from our feminist roots. Without trading in our dreams.

When I first asked this question at a meeting of the Society of Feminist Scholars and Their Friends, I was told to study the lay of the land. Several members politely added that as a philosopher who had made a lifelong study of education, I was a good person to do so. I took the advice, ultimately making three philosophical expeditions across the academy's terrain and submitting to the Society a rather technical report on each one. With the Society's blessing, I now present my findings to the general public.

CHAPTER 1

ESTRANGEMENT
FROM
EACH OTHER

On the day that I decided to turn the three reports on women in academe, which I had submitted to the Society of Feminist Scholars and Their Friends, into a report for the general public, I walked over to my tightly packed bookcase devoted to early feminist theory and pulled out a volume. The book is called *Sisterhood Is Powerful*. The publication date is 1970. Robin Morgan's introduction begins, "This book is an action. It was conceived, written, edited, copy-edited, proofread, designed, and illustrated by women."[1] The appendix contains a section called "Notes on Sister Contributors."[2] In 1998 I am stunned by the depth of the editor's commitment to the cause of women.

Next I dislodged Shulamith Firestone's *The Dialectic of Sex*, published that same year and dedicated to Simone de Beauvoir. I had forgotten how breathtaking this book is in scope and how bold its vision. I scan the discussions of Engels, Freud, love, ecology, racism, the myth of children and am struck anew by the brilliance of Firestone's synthesis.

The third book to catch my eye is *Voices of the New Feminism*, edited by Mary Lou Thompson. In this 1970 anthology Shirley Chisholm asks, "Will women dare in sufficient numbers to transform their own attitudes toward themselves and thus change the basic attitudes of males and the general society?"[3] And then I opened Adrienne Rich's 1976 volume *Of Woman Born*. "It is a book of revelations," says one reviewer. "The effect of this book is stunning," writes another. A third notes "the courage and intensity with which she writes."

Rich was a poet, Chisholm a congresswoman, Firestone a founder of the Women's Liberation Movement, Morgan a union organizer. Did feminist theory and research sever its connections to the women's movement, to women in the "outside" world, to activism when it began to be produced by members of the academy? Did it lose its passion? Was there a failure of nerve?

Not at first. The editors of the 1974 volume, *Women, Culture & Society* say in their preface: "By focusing on women, and by addressing facts that have conventionally been ignored or taken for granted, we hope to reappraise old theories and pave the way for future thought."[4] No failure of nerve here. In 1975 the editor of *Toward an Anthropology of Women* wrote: "This book has its roots in the women's movement. To explain and describe equality and inequality between the sexes, contemporary feminism has turned to anthropology with many questions in its search for a theory and a body of information. These questions are more than academic: the answers will help feminists in the struggle against sexism in our own society."[5] No severing of connections with activist roots yet. In 1978 Nancy Chodorow began the preface to *The Reproduction of Mothering* by saying, "This project owes its existence to the feminist movement and feminist community . . ."[6] In 1979 the editors of *The Prism of Sex* wrote: "These essays suggest that we must not only learn to ask new questions, but to challenge the very foundations on which the state of knowledge in each discipline is grounded."[7] That same year and in a similar vein, Susan Moller Okin, the author of *Women in Western Political Thought*, wrote: "The recent focus on women in the fields of history, legal studies, anthropology, sociology, and literary criticism has resulted in a number of innovative and important works, such that it is no exaggeration to say that these fields will never look the same again."[8]

In addition, in the early 1980s, there was the excitement of crucial feminist books from women of color: *This Bridge Called My Back,* edited by Cherrie Moraga and Gloria Anzaldúa; *All the Women are White, All Blacks Are Men, But Some of Us Are Brave,* edited by Gloria T. Hull, Patricia Bell Scott, and Barbara Smith; and the marvelous womanist essays written from 1967 to 1983 by Alice Walker, and published as *In Search of Our Mothers' Gardens.*

Hopes were high for the new scholarship on women, the dreams of a transformed knowledge and a transfigured world unbounded. And then things changed.

In the 1970s feminist scholars in the United States rarely criticized one another's work. Playing what has been called "the doubting game" where men's research was concerned, we played "the believing game" in relation to our own.[9] I now ask myself why we were so quick to adopt an acritical policy when self-criticism is one staff of a scholarly life. The answer is not hard to find. In a world in which women's words had for so long been discredited, the last thing we thought we needed was criticism from one another. Besides, in our eyes criticism represented conflict and we wanted to present a united front to the men who seemed so determined to undermine our efforts.

Having been schooled in philosophy, I belonged to a small minority who could not approve of an acritical—let alone an anti-critical—policy. Still, neither I nor anyone else was prepared for what happened in the 1980s. In that decade white feminist scholars took to self-criticism with a vengeance. In publications, and at meetings, workshops, and conferences we in the U.S. accused each other of essentialism on a regular basis. By decade's end, the list of those charged was a veritable *Who's Who* of feminism. Mary Daly and Adrienne Rich, two of the best-known feminist theorists of the day, were identified as essentialists and sightings were reported near the essentialist trap of such luminaries as Susan Griffith, Kathleen Barry, Janice Raymond, Susan Brownmiller, and Robin Morgan.[10]

I speak of accusations advisedly. If, in the 1980s, I had called a woman's research or she had called mine "essentialist," she or I would not merely have been offering criticism, as we would if we had called that work sketchy or unconvincing or disorganized or badly written or even false. We would have been placing on it an official seal of disapproval. When a literary scholar said, "You don't like to feel in a rank of things racist or sexist," her colleague asked, "Do they feel worse or better than being accused of being an essentialist?"[11] A prominent feminist theorist in turn said: "What I am very suspicious of is how anti-essentialism, really more than essentialism, is allowing women to call names and to congratulate ourselves."[12]

Just as the chilly coeducational classroom climate can inhibit women's intellectual development and kill our academic aspirations, a chilly atmosphere for women faculty can make us feel like alien beings who do not belong in the academy: a self-imposed chilly research climate can do women great harm. I had my first inkling of this the day I was asked to participate in a symposium commemorating the twentieth anniversary of the introduction of undergraduate coeducation at Princeton University. In my mind's ear I could hear feminist scholars warning me to think twice before agreeing to speak on the assigned topic, "The Gendered Voice in the Classroom." "*The* gendered voice?" sang one part of the chorus. "Do the people at that august institution actually believe that all women speak and think alike?" "The *gendered* voice?" replied another. "Don't they know that gender is an essentialist category?"

By early 1989 I had read too many books and articles by

women accusing other women of essentialism to want to attract such comments. Besides, scholars whose opinions I valued would not listen to my message were I to fall into the essentialist trap. I knew that one way to avoid the pitfall would be to shift my attention from the world of higher education to the symposium title. Methodologically speaking, I would have then been above reproach. However, this evasive strategy was at odds with my belief that women in higher education's classrooms are at risk, and that it is my obligation as a feminist scholar concerned with education to do what I can to alleviate their plight. Although my methodology might pass muster with my colleagues if I deconstructed the symposium title instead of the problems that women face in coeducational classrooms, according to my own lights I would be shirking my duty.

The policy I ultimately adopted for that Princeton symposium was to preface a paper about women in coeducational classrooms with a brief discussion of the pitfalls that a meeting about "the" gendered anything must try to avoid. So alarmed by my own timorous response to the Princeton invitation was I, however, that I promised myself to investigate the lay of the land more fully another time. Had I been especially thin-skinned, I might have thought no more about my initial impulse to flee the scene. But I am not. If the accusations of essentialism that feminist scholars directed at one another were making me think twice before speaking out, I felt compelled to find out what damage they might be doing to other feminist scholars.

The opportunity to make good on my vow soon came. Sitting in the cell-like office with dirty gray cinder-block walls and a spectacular view of Boston Harbor that I called my own, I had often asked myself what the accusations of essentialism were all about. What exactly did feminist scholars mean by essentialism, how did they think the new essentialism differed from the old, and why did one who fell into the essentialist trap become disabled? Forgetting my own advice to students—if you have a question but are afraid to speak because you think you will look dumb, ask it anyway for half the class is probably wondering the same thing—for years I had remained mute. The more charges of essentialism I came across, however, the more questions I had to suppress. The Society of Feminist Scholars and Their Friends had already encouraged me to explore the scholarly landscape. An invitation to attend an interdisciplinary conference in Canada on the topic of gender and knowledge offered me the occasion to discuss the lay of the land. To discuss it, I would first have to survey it. And so I sharpened my pencils, bought myself a stack of lined yellow pads, crammed some books into my briefcase and, pulling on my philosophical boots, set out on what turned out to be the first of three expeditions across the academy's terrain.

> > >

My official report on that journey contains a detailed description of the trap of essentialism that feminist scholars were flagging in the 1980s, a map of the neighboring territory, and charts of several unmarked scholarly pitfalls that my explorations had uncovered.[13] The question I want to raise here is the one a feminist literary scholar asked when her colleague informed her that at a conference on feminist theory held in the 1980s she had felt denounced and publicly dismissed.

"So what's at stake in these attacks?" demanded the scholar.[14] When I returned home from that first philosophical expedition, students in my feminist theory class asked the same question.

In an accusatory climate it is not easy to separate the tone of voice in which criticisms are expressed from their content. Yet it must be done, for part of what was at stake in these attacks was the understandable concern that feminist theorists were fanning

Western culture's prejudices toward women. The arguments put forward by all but a handful of the West's most respected thinkers had for more than two thousand years been premised on essences. Proceeding from assertions about women's essential nature to conclusions about our subordinate place in society and the legitimacy of men's domination over us, they read back onto our supposedly immutable, eternal essence or nature the social programs they claimed derive from it. Thus did philosophers, theologians, and other rational animals use essence talk to justify their own rule in both the family and the state.

When in the early 1980s feminist scholars began warning one another about the dangers of "the new essentialism," they were doing more than simply making implicit reference to the discredited project of arguing from women's nature to our place in society.[15] They were pointing out that some feminist theorists were trying to turn the tables on the men. They were saying that whereas proponents of the old essentialism attributed to women essential properties very different from and definitely *inferior* to those possessed by men, some contemporary feminist thinkers were representing us as possessing essential properties very different from and definitely *superior* to men's. Just as the men claimed to derive our moral, social, and political subordination from the inferior nature they mapped onto us, the women were claiming to derive our moral, social, and political superiority from the superior nature they assigned us.

What at first glance might seem a clever philosophical reversal is not to be condoned, said the feminist critics. Even though the content of the argument from women's nature has been changed, women are still the ones who stand to suffer. The skeptics maintained that the historical association between attributions of a female essence and women's imprisonment in the domestic "sphere" is so strong that any appeal to women's nature may well lead to a revival of the traditional Western view of women's proper place. They also insisted that feminist claims that women are caring and nurturing *by nature* support social and political programs that are inimical to women.

But if one thing at stake was that appeals to women's nature or essence can backfire on women, another thing was women's diversity. Although the entire time frame of the chilly research climate represents but a moment in the academy's history, there was a kind of temporal progression in the feminist criticisms of essentialism. They initially focused on the support that essences seem to lend programs and policies considered to harm women. But then, in the 1980s, white academic feminists in the United States began to recognize the terrible mistake that they—I should really say "we" for I fall into this category—had made in assuming that all the individuals in the world called "women" were alike. By the time I set out on my first philosophical expedition a new critique of essences had developed—one that singled out essentialism's masking of difference and diversity and the resulting illusion of uniformity.[16]

Feminist scholarship unquestionably stands to gain from the reminder that essence talk masks differences and that this masking can be destructive. There might be occasions on which an assumption of total uniformity does not matter. When, however, the subject is woman, false unity can definitely be— and undoubtedly has been—disabling. As the denial by male scholars of differences within the category of human beings led to the perception that women fall short of the norms of morality and mental health, to cite but two examples, the denial by female scholars of differences among women can cause some women to perceive other women as below standard or abnormal. Damaging self-confidence and destroying trust, essentialism can easily undermine efforts that aim at unified action.

The trouble is that, in seeking to avoid the trap of essentialism, feminist scholars began giving each other bad advice. Having learned in graduate school to be wary of talk about "man *as such*" because this sort of locution gives the impression that man has an essential nature, I sympathized from the start with those researchers and theorists who were telling each other to avoid talk of "womanhood" or "woman as such." But the critics also intimated that one who speaks of "gender identity" is committed to essentialism. And before long, they were saying that women and gender are themselves essentialist concepts or categories, and that reproduction and mothering are too.[17]

These categories are no more essentialist than chair, table, justice, or democracy. Consider the proceedings that we call "games," Ludwig Wittgenstein wrote in his *Philosophical Investigations:*

> I mean board-games, card-games, ball-games, Olympic games, and so on. What is common to them all?—Don't say: "There must be something common, or they would not be called 'games'"—but look and see whether there is anything common to all.—For if you look at them you will not see something that is common to all, but similarities, relationships, and a whole series of them at that.[18]

Wittgenstein went on to mention chess, tennis, naughts and crosses, ring-a-round-a-roses. "Similarities crop up and disappear" as we move from one group of games to the next, he continued, the result being that "we see a complicated network of similarities overlapping and criss-crossing: sometimes overall similarities, sometimes similarities of detail."

Wittgenstein referred to these complex relationships as "family resemblances."[19] What he did not do was tell us to stop calling those spectacularly diverse pastimes "games." That would be absurd. It would also be self-defeating for in the name of consistency we would have to ban the use of just about every general term. Yet in the 1980s feminist scholars tried to do something similar. They tried to extinguish the use of the very concepts that members of the professoriate had been loath to employ until those heady 1970s—the very concepts that feminist scholars had only just begun to use with such spectacular results.

The sad truth is that the feminist attack on women, gender, mothering, reproduction, and related concepts leaves feminist scholars in the lurch. In any field of inquiry imagination is at a premium. In a relatively new area, which feminist research is, the free play of imagination is especially important. In addition, in a field as young as ours, the development of diverse and even radically divergent research programs is to be desired. I can think of no better way to dampen the creative spirit or reduce interpretive diversity than to draw up a list of concepts to be avoided at all costs. Or rather, I can think of no better way to do this than to proscribe the very concepts that the new scholarship on women had only just begun to insert into the academy's vocabulary and at the same time to decide that feminist efforts to generalize about women's condition should be abandoned.

In the classic textbook case of false generalization, an inquirer generalizes about a whole population on the basis of an unrepresentative sample. There is no question that when women do this, the research can be disabling for women. bell hooks once wrote, "While it is in no way racist for any author to write a book exclusively about white women, it is fundamentally racist for books to be published that focus solely on the American white woman's experience in which that experience is assumed to be *the* American woman's experience."[20] She is absolutely right: in rendering other women invisible, this practice reduces their status "to that of non-person."[21] The practice is also politically damaging in that it separates women who might otherwise form fruitful alliances.

Feminist scholars were right to flag the trap of false generalization. It was the advice we then gave each other that I question. The obvious way for a scholar to keep from falsely generalizing is to make her sample more representative. Nevertheless, feminist theorists gave the impression that any attempt to replace a false generalization with a true one—or a more warranted generalization with a less warranted one—would be misguided. What should feminist scholars be doing instead of generalizing? We told one another to undertake studies that focus on difference and diversity—for instance, historical narratives of other times, anthropological reconstructions of other cultures, autobiographies, and oral histories.

In the heyday of the new scholarship on women, no one could have guessed that difference would emerge as the privileged perspective in feminist theory and research and that any attempt to find commonalties among women would be condemned out of hand. After all, it was the discovery that the experience of others was so like one's own that was at once comforting, illuminating, and energizing. Sadly, it turned out that this presumed discovery was a mere invention. Not only did we generalize from too homogeneous a sample; many of us assumed that those who are alike in some respects are alike in all. No one can say, however, that we white academic feminists, having found out how wrong we were, have been impenitent. Reporting sightings in or near the trap of false generalization of the most notable feminist thinkers of the day—among them Jean Baker Miller, Susan Brownmiller, Mary Daly, Robin Morgan, Shulamith Firestone, Michelle Rosaldo, Sherry Ortner, Carol Gilligan, Nancy Chodorow, and Catharine MacKinnon—we went on to condemn the consciousness-raising groups of the late 1960s and early 1970s, many of which were interracial, for leading women directly into the pitfall of false generalization.[22]

The self-imposed ban on generalizations rests on the

assumption that if women are different in some respects, they are different in all. Of course black and white women, middle-class and working-class women, Irish and Arab women are different. But just as no two individuals are alike in every respect, no two are different in every respect. The question of whether all women have one or more things in common cannot be answered in advance of investigation. Cutting us off from the developmental insights of feminist psychologists like Gilligan, Miller, and the authors of *Women's Ways of Knowing*, and denying us the chance to discover even limited cross-cultural and temporal commonalties, this trap encourages us to view not just other times and places but also other women as utterly Other.[23]

Philosopher Susan Bordo has written brilliantly about the a priori affirmation of difference by contemporary feminist theorists and has also remarked on "the coercive, mechanical requirement that all enlightened feminist projects attend to 'the intersection of race, class, and gender.'"[24] Add ethnicity, age, sexual orientation, and even then the list is incomplete. Prior to investigation how can anyone know that, in a woman's case, being a rape victim is not a difference that makes as much or perhaps far more difference than race or class? How do we know that, for us, difference does not turn on being fat or religious or in an abusive relationship?

Rightly responsive to charges of racism and classism and intent on avoiding the pitfall of false generalization, white feminist scholars ended up constructing for themselves the trap of predetermined categories. The fact that race and class have been considered fundamental variables in research about men scarcely entitles them in advance to the privilege these concepts now enjoy in the study of women. Nor does the existence of racist and classist practices within the academy accord them this status.

On the few occasions when I wondered aloud how we can be so sure that race and class are "the" fundamental variables in women's case, white middle-class feminist academics shrank from the question as from a born racist. Yet it is a mistake to assume that categories which apply in one field of action are necessarily the best ones to use in another.

I take the appallingly small percentage of nonwhite women in the professoriate to be a clear indication of institutional racism. Another sign is the paucity of curriculum content about the lives, works, and experiences of women of color, and one more is the underrepresentation of these women—as speakers at scholarly conferences, participants in scholarly symposia, and authors of chapters in scholarly anthologies.[25] But the fact that the concept or category of race illuminates the institutional practices of a racist society does not automatically make it a fruitful explanatory category for every theoretical inquiry. Although her sample was not all white, I have heard Gilligan's research on the different moral voice called racist more times than I can count. Yet until the relevant research is done there is no way of knowing if the different voice Gilligan brought to our attention belongs to white girls and women only or if it is, so to speak, a cross-race voice. We simply do not know if in this case race—or, for that matter, class, ethnicity, or sexual orientation—is a difference that makes a difference.

Even more troubling than the "coercive mechanical requirement" that feminist research must always and everywhere attend to race and class, said Bordo, "is the (often implicit, sometimes explicit) dogma that the only 'correct' perspective on race, class, and gender is the affirmation of difference."[26] Actually, however, even as feminist theorists told us to lay bare the diversity that exists within the category of women, they manufactured unity within the more specific racial and class categories. Regarding being black, for example, as "the" defining property of black women, diverse feminists lost sight of the myriad ways in which black women differ from one another. Reasoning that if one property—e.g., being black or Asian—is held in common by women then all properties are, they compounded the invalid inference that all black or Asian women are utterly different from all white women by the equally fallacious one that all black or all Asian women are absolutely alike.

What could be more dangerous for women than to disregard similarities when different categories of women are being compared? What could be more self-defeating than to see no differences within these categories? These strategies accomplish the very thing that feminist scholars have wanted to avoid—representing women who belong to another race or class as the Other. They also legitimate an analog in feminist scholarship to the old "separate but equal" segregationist policy. When, not so long ago, feminist scholars exposed the male bias of men's scholarship, we said that when women are brought into the disciplines of knowledge, new narratives and theories will have to be constructed. But when feminist scholarship itself was charged with race and class bias, our response was different. Proclaiming in advance the impossibility of constructing adequate "integrated" theories and narratives, feminist theorists opted for a "different but equal" policy.

Assume that black and white women or middle-class and working-class women are radically different, and there is no point in telling a feminist scholar who has generalized falsely to improve her sample. For given this premise, no matter what she does the only generalizations she can come up with will be false. The assumption of absolute difference is untenable, however, and the best that can be said about the presumption that when the missing women are finally brought into feminist research scholars must treat them separately—that, in effect, there should be no intermingling of races or classes—is that it is intellectually stifling.

I do not condemn studies of difference or indict ones that segregate different categories of women for the purpose of study. One thing I learned on my first tour of the terrain is that the field of feminist theory and research has been greatly enriched by work of this very sort. Another is that such research might never have been undertaken—or, if undertaken, might not have been published—had not we white academic feminist scholars acknowledged our mistakes. It is not one or the other kind of scholarship but the either/or approach to understanding social life that I reject here.

> ❯ ❯ ❯

So what's at stake in these attacks? From the point of view of those making the accusations, at stake in women scholars' self-policing was the deep-seated fear that our own research would unwittingly reinforce Western culture's stereotyped vision of women and a genuine desire to rid our theories and ourselves of racist tendencies. From the standpoint of the growth and development of the field of feminist scholarship itself, at stake was methodological advice that stunts feminist inquiry and promotes a view of women who differ from oneself as utterly Other. At stake, too, was the timidity and the estrangement of feminist scholars from one another that a culture of fear produces.

At meetings, workshops, and conferences I attended upon my return home from my first philosophical expedition, I heard rumors that the debate about essentialism was dead. Yet as the decade progressed, brand-new sightings near the essentialist trap were reported and meanwhile the old ones were being broadcast abroad. Citing the time lag between the publication of feminist theory and research in North America and its availability in Scandinavia, a Swedish philosopher told me in 1995 that in her country accusations of essentialism were then a relatively common occurrence. She also informed me that unconfirmed reports of the old sightings were being handed down to the next generation of feminist scholars and being taken as gospel. "Why should I bother reading Carol Gilligan when she is essentialist? Why would I waste my time on essentialists like Mary Daly and Adrienne Rich?" the new feminist scholars were saying. When one considers that the women who stood accused were among the best known and most widely read feminist scholars of the time, this easy indifference is perhaps the greatest irony of them all.

But suppose the accusations stop. The research climate will not improve if academic feminists continue to fall into the trap of a double standard. The feminist scholars who originally flagged this trap sighted men in its neighborhood, but on my first philosophical expedition I saw women congregating there in record numbers. It had become a feminist fashion to look tolerantly upon the gravest mistakes and omissions of a Michel, a Jacques, a Jean-Francois, while denouncing works by women that contained far less egregious errors.

Take Michel Foucault. Feminist scholars have made devastating criticisms of his work on sexuality for, among other things, ignoring women's writings and denying power differences in male-female relationships in his approach to rape law.[27] Do critiques like these lead feminist theorists to dismiss his work? Not at all. They tell us that it is a rich source of understanding and empowerment. I agree that feminists can learn much from Foucault, Derrida, and others. We need to do some soul-searching, however, about the discrepancy between our cordial treatment of the men's theories and our punitive approach to the women's.

Many prominent contemporary feminist scholars have been accused of essentialism. Perhaps no one, however, has so frequently and from so many quarters been charged with falling into the traps of essentialism and false generalization as Gilligan.[28] Upon realizing that the original samples leading to Gilligan's discovery of a different voice[29] were limited, her readers had ample reason to conclude that she had not demonstrated that women of all races and classes spoke in that different voice. Feminist critics instead convicted her of false unity. Knowing that Gilligan was a psychologist, not a historian, readers also had excellent grounds for judging that she had not shown that the different voice existed in historical periods other than our own. Feminist theorists instead condemned her for being ahistorical. Pointing to the various ways in which Gilligan's discovery had still to be confirmed or disconfirmed, feminist scholars could have treated it as a hypothesis. Instead, they left the impression that further research was unnecessary. They implied, if they did not actually say, that Gilligan's ahistorical approach demonstrated the nonexistence of the different voice in other times and without taking the trouble to find out that her sample included black middle-class women and white working-class women, they intimated that its limited nature proved that the voice was uniquely white and middle class.

In the event, the accusations and the application of a double standard did not cause Gilligan to abandon her research program.[30] Yet who knows what it might have done to others? Who can begin to measure the timidity it produced?

Echoing the high hopes of U.S. feminist scholars in the 1970s, a Norwegian philosopher asked in 1995 "How do we make a more lasting impact, how do we make women's research part of a common heritage?"[31] A self-policing that kills our courage, silences our voices, and restricts our vision is not the way. We need to be open to intellectual possibilities and receptive to different ideas, including those formulated by feminist scholars. It is fine to fill in the gender gaps in the theories of Foucault and the others so long as we do as much for ourselves: so long as we take other women's academic work seriously enough to criticize it constructively; so long as we encourage and participate in its further development and elaboration; so long as we consider the possibility of integrating it into our own thinking. For to maintain the double standard is to replace the dream of transforming both knowledge and the world through our scholarship with the self-abnegating goal of insuring the theoretical adequacy of the men's ideas.

> ❭ ❭ ❭

What price belonging? Can feminist scholars find acceptance in the academy without losing sight of our mothers, daughters, sisters, half-sisters, female cousins, and aunts? Can we find it without becoming divided from our past, present, and future selves?

I set out on my first philosophical expedition into the academic workplace at the very time when women's studies programs had begun to bloom in the U.S. academy and women's professional societies to flourish in the various academic disciplines. Who can blame feminist scholars for thinking that the day when we too would be accepted in the academy was drawing nigh! At this historical juncture I saw white feminist scholars:

> ❭ turn their backs on their sister scholars—all in the name of anti-essentialism;
>
> ❭ construct walls around feminists of different races—all in the name of honoring diversity;
>
> ❭ and recommend research practices that, if followed, would stunt the growth and development of their own field of inquiry.

CHAPTER II

ESTRANGEMENT FROM WOMEN'S LIVED EXPERIENCE

The interdisciplinary conference on gender and knowledge was held in Calgary in June 1991. One year later I attended an international conference on girls and girlhood—the very first of its kind. On the plane home from Amsterdam I wrote myself a long letter about the forgotten world of girls and women. I also jotted down on my calendar a reminder to reread Carol Cohn's hair-raising essay.

In "Sex and Death in the Rational World of Defense Intellectuals" Cohn told of her experiences at a 1984 workshop on nuclear arms control. As she learned the language of the defense intellectuals she found that her own thinking was becoming more abstract, was focusing on "parts disembedded from their context," was attending more to the survival of weapons than human beings.[1] Calling this educational experience transformative, Cohn outlined the quandary facing those who opposed the then U.S. nuclear policy: "If we refuse to learn the language, we are virtually guaranteed that our voices will remain outside the 'politically relevant' spectrum of opinion. Yet, if we do learn and speak it, we not only severely limit what we can say but we also invite the transformation, the militarization, of our own thinking."[2]

It occurred to me on first reading the Cohn article that her quandary represented a more general problem. After that Amsterdam conference I felt sure my hunch was correct. Generalize Cohn's problem and what have we got? A fundamental dilemma—perhaps *the* fundamental one—of higher education.

"If I spoke English rather than expert jargon," Cohn reported, "the men responded to me as though I were ignorant, simpleminded, or both."[3] In the academy, as in the defense establishment, to speak plain English is to appear ignorant and simpleminded. "I entered a world where people spoke what amounted to a foreign language, a language I had to learn if we were to communicate with one another," she wrote.[4] When you enter an academic institution you also walk into a world in which languages you do not understand are spoken. To communicate with the defense intellectuals Cohn had to learn to decode acronyms like SRAM (short-range attack missile) and use phrases such as "collateral damage" and "subholocaust engagement." To talk to philosophers one must be able to decode phrases such as "the ontological argument," "necessary and sufficient conditions," and "the Cartesian ego"; pronounce words like "epistemological," "deontological," and "modal"; and understand "borderline case," "bad faith," and other idioms. To converse with psychologists one must comprehend the likes of "operant conditioning," "reaction formation," "transference," and "cognitive dissonance." And one must, of course, address chemists, biologists, sociologists, economists, and literary critics in their own tongues.

To her dismay, Cohn discovered that despite its grizzly subject matter the words of "technostrategic," the language she had to learn, "are fun to say; they are racy, sexy, snappy. You can throw them around in rapid-fire succession. They are quick, clean, light; they trip off the tongue."[5] I get the definite impression that those fluent in psychoanalysis feel the same way about "cathexis," "defense mechanism," "narcissism," and "instinctual object choice." Those fluent in economics, in turn, seem pleased to say "utility maximization," "consumption choices," "competitive equilibrium," and "gains-from-trade model." And just as in Cohn's experience nearly everyone appeared to take pleasure in using the words of technostrategic, in mine nearly everyone who has learned the language of philosophy seems to enjoy employing its specialized vocabulary.

Cohn found that technostrategic language's appeal lay in "the thrill of being able to manipulate an arcane language, the power of entering the secret kingdom, being someone in the know."[6] As a philosophy student I experienced that same thrill and one more. Cohn marveled that by the time you are through learning technostrategic language, "the content of what you can talk about is monumentally different, as is the perspective from which you speak."[7] Once I learned the academic language of philosophy, I spoke and thought about new things, asked questions that would never before have occurred to me, and envisioned possibilities that previously had not entered my mind. More than this, my perspective on the world was different.

George Eliot once wrote: "Perspective, as its inventor remarked, is a beautiful thing. What horrors of damp huts, where human beings languish, may not become picturesque through aerial distance! What hymning of cancerous vices may we not languish over as sublimest art in the safe remoteness of a strange language and artificial phrase!"[8] Cohn's account of becoming fluent in technostrategic language matches Eliot's description of aerial distance.

Cohn's perspective changed, and with it her cognitive landscape. Even as her new tongue enabled her to talk about things she had not been able to discuss before, it "radically excluded" other topics and concerns.[9] But for this last fact, there would have been no quandary. If in order to communicate in the world of defense intellectuals Cohn had merely to master a foreign language, she would not have faced an unpleasant choice. However, the topics and concerns that the new tongue excluded were the very issues that had driven her to learn it in the first place: peace, human death, the destruction of human societies. My own experience with the language of philosophy made it impossible for me, in turn, to ask the very questions about curriculum which had so troubled me as a grade-school teacher that I had turned for answers to the field of philosophy—indeed, I could scarcely recall the values that had sent me into school teaching in the first place.

Besides excluding talk about the urgent issues of human destruction and peace, Cohn's new language placed speakers at a far remove from whatever pressing matters they did find it possible to discuss.[10] Thus, a defense intellectual described the aftermath of a nuclear attack as "a situation bound to include EMP blackout, brute force damage to systems, a heavy jamming environment, and so on."[11] From his perspective the figures looming up "hairless and faceless," the screams "with voices that were no longer human," and the groans "rising everywhere from the rubble," as depicted by Japanese survivors, are not perceptible.

The languages of the academy also place its speakers at an aerial distance from the world's ills. Susan Schaller, the author of *A Man Without Words* asked, "How could such a gulf exist between the universities and the streets? How could a researcher consider a prelingual deaf adult learning language a once-in-a-lifetime happening, when four were sitting at the same table only a few miles away?"[12]

Making it impossible to see the pain and suffering that accompany real-life phenomena—or, if these be seen, to feel the attendant horrors—the aerial distance achieved by those who speak the languages of the academy desensitizes our thinking. It can also render us callous toward the victims of such "cancerous vices" as poverty and disease, domestic violence and sexual abuse, racism and sexism, global war and environmental destruction.

Virginia Woolf pictured the educated men on her bridge in Shakespearean terms as human beings "sans teeth, sans eyes, sans taste, sans everything." Psychiatrist Robert J. Lifton has coined the term "psychological numbing" for the diminished capacity or inclination to feel and to imagine what will happen that is exhibited by those who do not fully contemplate or comprehend the consequences of nuclear war.[13] A dampening of feeling and suppression of moral imagination is the price paid by those who fall into the trap of aerial distance.

Academic jargon and aerial distance: these are not by-products of feminist self-policing. They are basic mores of the academy. Nevertheless, the fact that the members of academe are supposed to conform to them does not mean that feminist scholars can do so with impunity: without severing ourselves from our roots in the Women's Movement, without rejecting the claims of sisterhood.

Cohn's paper made me think that if feminists do not speak one or more of the technical languages found in the academy— or, alternatively, if we do not construct our own exotic tongues—we will appear ignorant or simpleminded. And then it is virtually guaranteed that our voices will not be heard within the academy's walls; or, if heard, that they will not be attended to. So we have little choice but to speak expert jargon rather than plain English. Yet, one who speaks even a feminist-inspired academese is at great risk of seeing the lived world through aerial distance. When, roughly a year after that conference in Amsterdam, an editor of the feminist scholarly journal *Signs* wrote, "How imitative are we of the academic establishment in which we have been trained, against which we have often raised objections, and in which most of us are now also so invested?"[14], I knew the time had come to make a second philosophical expedition across the scholarly terrain.

❯ ❯ ❯

It goes without saying that in trying to secure a place in the academy many, probably most, feminist scholars have learned to speak one or more forms of academese. Almost every scholar must do so. Indeed, no sooner did I hang a "Back Later" sign on my office door than I began to hear colleagues throw around in rapid-fire succession phrases such as "a monologic masculinist economy," "the cultural construction of subjectivity," "radical nominalism," and "feminist interrogation," and derive great pleasure from saying "the tripartite axis of power-knowledge-pleasure," "the interpellation of the subject," "the displacement of modernism by postmodernism," and "the genealogy of the essentializing discourse."

Of course, it is quite possible to speak expert jargon without losing sight of the lived world. I think of my physician, who, although fluent in medicalese, speaks plain English to me. Nevertheless, Cohn's experience demonstrates how easy it is to fall into the trap of aerial distance. And my own firsthand experience of the trap bears this out. When as a fifth-grade teacher I decided that I had to do something about the boring, mindless, disconnected curriculum I was expected to teach my students, I was brought up short by the arbitrariness of my attempts at reform. What justified my thinking that the social studies curriculum I was designing was better than the one in place? How did a person rationally decide what content to include and when? Once I discovered analytic philosophy, I knew that to answer my own questions I would have to continue my studies. The trouble was that the more fluent I became in the language of philosophy, the more distant seemed the problems that had once exercised me.

Cohn confessed that she had to struggle to climb out of the "rabbit hole" she had fallen down.[15] Judging from my own experience, she made a quick escape from the trap of aerial distance. Perhaps she was able to do so because she was not, and never wished to become, a bona fide member of the community of defense intellectuals. A British sociologist of knowledge has said, the dominant characteristic of high-status knowledge is that it is "'at odds' with daily life and common experience."[16] He was discussing his own nation's education, but he might just as well have been talking about the stratification of knowledge in the United States. In both cultures the academy follows the tacit rule that the more removed from everyday experience, the better the knowledge. And in the United States, as in many other nations, the academy also operates on a principle of guilt by association. Other things being equal, a person's status derives from the status of the knowledge that she or he produces.

With no stake in the defense intellectual community, Cohn could distance herself relatively easily from the aerial distance it so prized. However, I know all too well from my own experience that a man or woman whose fervent wish is to belong in the academy can take a long time just to acknowledge the existence of the aerial distance trap and even longer to start trying to escape it.

To flag the aerial distance trap, as I do here, is not to deplore every inquiry in which a feminist investigator fails to merge with her subject matter. In the first place, total identification is illusory. More important, just as aerial distance can cause one to lose sight of the everyday world, the attempt to close the gap between a scholar and her objects of study can have untoward effects. "When you come right down to it," Robert Oppenheimer said about the building of the atomic bomb, "the reason that we did this job is because it was an organic necessity. If you are a scientist you cannot stop such a thing. If you are a scientist you believe that it is good to find out how the world works; that it is good to find out what the realities are."[17] Apparently, Oppenheimer was so close to the project he brilliantly carried to completion that he could not see around or beyond it. This myopia allowed him to transform a question about death and destruction, war and peace, into one about the inviolability of scientific curiosity. Compare the perspective that Cohn attained on the defense intellectuals' project with Oppenheimer's on his own. After getting close enough to her subjects of study to explain the appeal of technostrategic speech, Cohn stepped far enough back from them to construct a critique, even an exposé, of their language and their world.

If aerial distance is a trap and if too little distance can be just as dangerous, in what relation to her objects of study should a feminist scholar stand? There is no general rule for us to follow, other than "It all depends." In some contexts the attempt to get as close as possible to one's objects of study will be the best policy. In others we may be well advised to gain some distance from our subject matter. Moreover, although different objects of study may on any given occasion call for different treatments, there is no reason to think that each will always demand the same kind of treatment. An object that in one context is best served by distance may in another benefit most from closeness.

At the Amsterdam conference, however, overidentification with one's research objects was not an issue for the accusations of essentialism and false generalization that had led many, many feminist scholars to focus on their own methodologies. I fully agree with those who have said that the turn to methodology effectively diverted attention away from the very racist, classist, and other exclusionary practices of the academy that feminist academics had been deploring.[18] But it had another untoward consequence as well. The new fascination with methodology represented a turn away from the lived lives of girls and women. Just as the analytic philosophy I learned to do in graduate school distanced me from the everyday problems of education by focusing my attention on language to the exclusion of pressing educational issues, the concern with methodology distances feminist scholars from the actual problems facing women in the everyday world.

I cannot say too strongly that I am not issuing a wholesale condemnation of feminist studies of language or methodologies. My point is that to focus on these is to turn one's attention away from the problems of the real world. If self-reflection helps feminist scholars see the world more clearly, the time may be well spent. To bring this point home, I can only hope that the self-reflections I report here are so justified. To my mind, the issue is one of balance: balance not in an individual scholar's own inquiries but within the field of feminist scholarship as a whole. Actually, because we can never know in advance what any given bit of research is going to shed light on, I believe that space should be reserved within the field of feminist scholarship for aerial distance work, be it self-reflective or not. I worry, however, lest so many feminist scholars become addicted to self-reflection that aerial distance becomes the norm.

For the record, let me emphasize that aerial distance and esotericism are separate pitfalls: a scholar who steps into the aerial distance trap maintains too great a distance from her objects of study whereas one who falls into the esotericist trap maintains too great a distance from her audience. Because esotericism, like aerial distance, is standard academic practice, it is not surprising that feminist scholars who seek acceptance have fallen into this trap. Yet as editors of the feminist publication *Transformations* have said, "The use of jargon excludes people from the 'conversation.' "[19] In particular, it keeps the knowledge constructed by feminist scholars—the narratives, theories, analyses we produce—out of the hands of feminist activists and away from the untold numbers of women who work with women and girls on a daily basis. Thus, just as aerial distance can prevent feminist scholarship from guiding or even informing feminist practice because it does not address the concerns of activists or confront the issues that presently cry out for remediation, esotericism can have the same effect because no one except a small circle of scholars can understand what is being said.

Because feminist scholars speak so many different expert languages and no one can possibly learn them all, esotericism also keeps feminists inside the academy from understanding each other. I once asked an acquaintance if she had enjoyed the public lecture we had both attended. "I didn't understand a word," she replied. And then, to assure me that she was not criticizing the feminist speaker she added: "Of course, it's my fault. I was trained in psychology and sociology, not philosophy." I tried to say that since this lecture was meant for the public it was the speaker's fault, not hers, but she seemed anxious to take the blame. The *Signs* editorial said, "In the effort to give ourselves the prestige we seek . . . we may also try to align ourselves with those who represent High Theory, which speaks a language not known for its accessibility."[20] Here was as clear-cut an example of the way the trap of esotericism reinforces hierarchy as one might wish.

On my second philosophical expedition I heard esoteric language defended as the inevitable byproduct of sophisticated thinking. This is the same argument I encountered at a workshop on education I once attended. When two participants referred to another woman there as the only feminist theorist present, I reminded them that I did feminist theory—indeed had been doing it at that very meeting. Their instant reply was, "You cannot possibly be a feminist theorist. We can understand what you say." The previous day, the woman whose credentials as a theoretician were not in doubt had defended her own esotericism by declaring that you cannot construct feminist theory—indeed, any kind of theory—if you do not speak a form of expert jargon. Her message actually seemed to be that the more technical the language, the better the theory. The renowned sociologist Pierre Bourdieu relies on an assumption very like this when in defense of his own esotericism he says that only a complex discourse can do justice to complex phenomena.[21]

Now I do not believe that Bourdieu is right, but suppose that theory construction does indeed require the use of esoteric language. We still do not face the unpleasant choice: use inaccessible language or avoid theory. Esotericism is not so much a matter of *using* technical language as of *misusing* it. Thus, if theory and technical language really are inextricably connected, theory can still be communicated successfully to the uninitiated.

Failing to discriminate between the use of technical language in theory construction or development and its use in communicating theory to others, feminists who fall into the esotericist trap indiscriminately use technical language in both contexts. But a feminist or any other kind of scholar need not do this because the possibility of "translating" the theory's esoteric language always exists. True, a translator of expert jargon into ordinary English must be willing to settle for something less than completeness. She must agree, in effect, that a scholar does not have to say to every audience exactly what she would say to fluent speakers of her expert jargon. Granted, it is not always easy for one who speaks an expert jargon to match her level of discourse to her audience's. Of course, things can get lost in translation. But happily, if what is omitted or simplified or passed over quickly in one context counts as a loss—and it does not always—that particular concept or idea or nuance can be regained in other contexts.

As I list here the dangers attaching to the esoteric language trap, I marvel that feminist scholars have not cordoned off the area. Then I remember that the assumption that most feminist academics will automatically want to reconnect their theorizing with the activities of the real world does not reckon with the academy's value system.

Bourdieu has pointed out that one device for accumulating reputation in the academy is an "elevated" style.[22] True, his subject is the French academy, but the analysis holds good for the British and North American cases as well. Moreover, in these instances, as well as the French, two other devices for accumulating reputation loom large: the abstractness of the knowledge or research and its unrelatedness to daily life.[23]

Why these signs of status and not, for instance, the concreteness of knowledge, its relatedness to daily life, or its accessible style? One of the books I took with me on my second expedition was Thorstein Veblen's *The Higher Learning in America*. Writing in 1906 that only in the several generations just past had the higher learning in the United States become an avowed end in itself, Veblen said, "The affairs of life, except the affairs of learning, do not touch the interest of the university man as a scholar or scientist."[24] Aware of how much things have changed since Veblen produced his analysis—after all, the arts and sciences are now peopled by men *and* women who find that the affairs of life affect their research at every turn—I considered leaving this volume behind. I have since come to believe, however, that in broad outline Veblin's account still holds true.

Yes, academicians today deplore the inroads of the marketplace into their domain. Yes, policy studies have proliferated in academe. On the other hand, at an international conference on scientific research held in Norway in 1995 a noted scholar from the U.S. answered a question about the practical import of his research by saying "If I were interested in making the world better I wouldn't have become a sociologist. I'm not a social worker or a priest. I don't care what uses my work is put to. I entered the field to answer certain questions." A few months later, a writer for the *Boston Globe* said: "These days, the search for solutions to the problems that confront American society leads to policy foundations and thoughtful periodicals far more often than to its colleges and universities."[25]

But my main concern is not whether Veblen's insight into the academy remains valid. Suppose it does not: suppose that the academy today does value the everyday world of practice. In assuming that there is a one-way street between thought and action, the academy misrepresents that world's relationship to theory. The academy takes it for granted that theory has great benefits to bestow on practice—illumination, for one thing, and guidance, for another—but denies that practice has anything to offer in return. [26]

This idea of the theory/practice relationship fits together nicely with the academy's self-definition as an institution having as few dealings as possible with the everyday world. Indeed, it allows academy members to pursue theoretical knowledge while letting the chips fall where they may. But the presumed asymmetry between theory and practice obscures the potential of feminist practice to inform feminist theory and even serve as its source. In establishing a hierarchical relationship in which feminist theory is the dominant and feminist practice the subordinate partner, the assumption of a one-way street between thought and action also leads to the valuing of feminist scholars and theoreticians over feminist activists and practitioners.

I will never forget the time a group of local feminist peace workers showed a film about their organization and its activities to the women's studies faculty of the university I happened to be visiting. As I sat admiring the courage of nonviolent women who were daily risking arrest, injury, and perhaps even death, and marveling at how much feminist academics could learn from these activists, scholarly hands shot up. "Why do I see only middle-class women in your film?" asked one feminist scholar. "Nonviolent tactics cannot succeed in the world today," commented another. The divorce of feminist scholarship from feminist activism and the presumed superiority of the former had never been made so plain to me.[27]

Feminist theorist Charlotte Bunch may have exaggerated when in 1979 she affirmed that "in all aspects of theory development, theory and activism continually inform and alter each other."[28] But her thesis that theory "both grows out of and guides activism in a continuing spiraling process"[29]—one that philosophers like John Dewey would say holds good for all theory—is still compelling. The academy's vision of the theory/practice relationship, on the other hand, harks back to Plato's antidemocratic political philosophy. In the Just State of Plato's *Republic*, only a special few are sufficiently rational to grasp the extremely theoretical kind of knowledge deemed genuine. The moral, social, and political decisions affecting the lives of the multitude are, therefore, to be made by an intellectual elite who are duty-bound to use it wisely on behalf of all others. In principle, although certainly not in actuality, all citizens of a democracy are participants in governing—equal participants, at that. This means that if a democratic government is to be wise rather than foolish, knowledge relating to existing policies and practices as well as to possible future alternatives must be widely distributed, not kept in the hands of the initiated few. It also means that no group has a privileged relationship to "the" truth.

In short, the devaluation of the practices and problems of the everyday world that is implicit in the academy's biased view of the theory/practice relationship is both elitist and divisive. Representing academicians as a special kind of professional from whom even the most experienced and professional practitioners must seek guidance, this model reinstates the very sort of inegalitarianism that the women's movement—the movement from which feminist scholarship sprang—set out to abolish.

> > >

I returned to my office from my second philosophical expedition a sobered woman. When I was a graduate student, arguments for and against essentialism were part of the official curriculum of my chosen subject, philosophy, and I was left to draw my own conclusions. In contrast, I acquired my favorable attitudes toward aerial distance and esotericism from the academy's hidden curriculum. For many, many years I was deeply suspicious of those few philosophers who wrote and spoke in a language that everyone could understand, and I harbored the unshakable conviction that good philosophy was not supposed to shed light on everyday problems. Beliefs and prejudices that you do not know you acquired in school but that have become part and parcel of your identity are very hard to discard, especially when there are few incentives for doing so and the risks are great. Where the academy is concerned, no one wants to be drummed out of her discipline, which can happen if you focus on what is held to be inappropriate subject matter. No one wants her work ignored, which is a strong possibility if you make it so accessible as to be deemed simplistic.

I would not be surprised to learn that the tales of our acceptance by the academy are a bit exaggerated: as were the early accounts of the integration of the new scholarship on women into the liberal curriculum; as, indeed, was Woolf's pronouncement in 1932 that the originality of Mary Wollstonecraft's philosophy of women's rights and women's education "has become our commonplace."[30] I realize too that those who struggle for acceptance may not judge it to be in their best interests to speak out against the academy's basic mores or to act counter to them. Yet for us to bask in the escapist atmosphere that the academy constructs out of aerial distance, esotericism, and the devaluation of the practical is to cut ourselves off from our activist roots. With the everyday world all but forgotten and the reality of women's and girls' lives blocked out; with communication between us and women outside the academy all but severed: we will be divided from our own raison d'être.

While I was out mapping the terrain, antifeminists back home were telling all and sundry that statistics on rape are wildly exaggerated, research on high school girls' plummeting self-esteem is laughable, the math gap between U.S. boys and girls is negligible, and hardly anyone dies from anorexia nervosa.[31] Upon my return I worried—in fact, I am still worried—

that even as antifeminist women in the academy *say* that the horrors that have only recently been seen and named do not exist, all too many of us *act as if* they do not.

How ironic that we academic feminists have so removed ourselves from the problems and practices of everyday life that we need to start telling one another, much as Abigail Adams told her husband, John, to remember the ladies! Yet this is the academy's admission price.

What's at stake here? The first way of being at ease in a "world," Maria Lugones has said, is being a fluent speaker in that world, and a second way is to agree with its norms.[32] The trouble with our being at ease in academe is that the academy's admission price includes an aerial distance that renders the lives of girls and women unseen; an esotericism that divides women in the academy from the women and girls standing outside its doors; and a devaluation of the practical that separates feminist scholars from feminist activists. And then there is a conception of theory that divides feminist theorists from feminist practitioners.

Once one has grown accustomed to the academy's escapist atmosphere it is easy to ignore this exorbitant membership fee. However, those 1970s books on my shelf testify that to include us on the academy's rosters is a small price for the patriarchy to pay to keep us from doing scholarship that might "challenge the very foundations on which the state of knowledge in each discipline is grounded" and "pave the way for future thought." I need only recall that those early academic feminists wanted to "help feminists in the struggle against sexism in our own society" to know that in giving us professorships and offices of our own, the patriarchy is paying a mere pittance to keep the knowledge we acquire from falling into the hands of feminist activists and practitioners.

In our eagerness to belong, we have traded in those dreams of the 1970s. Yet, what options does a feminist scholar have?

Cohn put her quandary in either/or terms: you refuse to learn defensese, in which case your voice is not heard, or you learn the language, in which case your thinking is transformed. Now that we have gained—or at least are in the process of gaining—acceptance in the academy, it would be sad indeed for us to decide, as Bunch once did, that the only way to join thought to action is to leave scholarship behind us. It is equally egregious, however, to be co-opted by the academy. Fortunately, there is another alternative, albeit one fraught with difficulties: we can work to change the academy's atmosphere by resisting and subverting its escapist practices.

The fact that the academy defines itself as the home of thought divorced from action and of theory uninformed by practice does not mean that this definition of its mission cannot change. Nor does the fact that we are being accepted into the academy mean that, feeling forever grateful to those who tried so hard to keep us out, we must now accede to even its most undemocratic and inegalitarian tendencies. There is no reason—apart from the excellent one of the very real dangers to our own careers—why we cannot in good conscience direct our *collective* energies to changing the academy's core values and its basic mores of aerial distance and esoteric language.

I stress "collective" because we can succeed in bringing about the needed reforms only if we all work together. But I also underline the importance of understanding the conditions of our employment—the practices, norms, and ideology that constitute the institution we seek to reform—and of deconstructing their gendered aspects.

Philosopher Sandra Harding has said that science "excludes itself from the categories and activities it prescribes for everything else. It recommends that we understand everything but science through causal analyses and critical scrutiny of inherited beliefs."[33] Education also excludes itself from the categories and activities it prescribes. Bidding those who come under its sway to go forth and understand, it teaches that just about everything is a legitimate object of understanding except itself. "The project that science's sacredness makes taboo is the examination of science in just the ways any other institution or set of social practices can be examined," wrote Harding.[34] Education also manages to foreclose examination of its own presuppositions.

Harding has argued for an "external" understanding of science that goes beyond—or gets behind—consciously held scientific beliefs to seek an understanding of science's gendered aspects. The academy and the larger educational system to which it belongs require a similar kind of understanding. This does not mean that every feminist scholar should do educational research. It does, however, mean that feminist scholars need to start taking the academy seriously as a bona fide object of study. This, in turn, means placing ourselves at sufficient distance from the practices and belief systems we have inherited—although not an aerial distance that renders them invisible—to be able to reflect critically on them.

Bunch had the outside, everyday world very much in mind when in 1979 she offered her defense of feminist theory. I like to think that even in the skeptical, cynical years that mark the onset of the twenty-first century we academic feminists can recapture something very like her concern for that world. We can only do so, however, if we keep our eyes on the need to change the world of the academy in which we now live. Ignorance of the academy's mores and ideology all but guarantees the failure of any such attempt.

❯　❯　❯

What price belonging? Can feminist scholars find acceptance in the academy without losing sight of our mothers, daughters, sisters, half-sisters, female cousins, and aunts? Can we find it without becoming divided from our past, present, and future selves?

On my first philosophical expedition into the academic workplace I learned that feminist scholars were becoming divided from one another. On this field trip I saw feminist scholars:

> turn their backs on the problems confronting women in the "real" world—in the name of aerial distance;

> separate themselves from feminist activists and from one another—in the name of esotericism;

> and place themselves above feminist activists and practitioners of all kinds—in the name of a one-sided theory/practice relationship.

CHAPTER III

ESTRANGEMENT FROM "WOMEN'S" OCCUPATIONS

In the decade when the hopes of feminist scholars were high, education was a major feminist concern. In the 1970s discoveries of sex-role stereotypes in children's readers, arithmetic workbooks, and social studies texts fueled our anger. Revelations of salary differentials, the underrepresentation of women in school and college administration, the budget gap between men's and women's intercollegiate sports spurred us to action. When the androcentric, Eurocentric cast of one after another discipline of knowledge was demonstrated, we debated whether to establish separate women's studies programs or integrate the study of women across the subjects of the liberal curriculum and poured our energies into constructing theories of curricular transformation. When the chilly climate of the coeducational college classroom was documented, we inquired into the merits of single-sex schooling and compiled accounts of feminist pedagogy.

In that same decade Adrienne Rich published several short essays that cast new light on women's higher education. But then a funny thing happened. Except for bell hooks, who has consistently paid attention to education, and for the precious few who defined themselves—I should really say ourselves—as scholars of education, feminist academics lost interest.

Searching my bookshelves for examples of contemporary feminist theory that give education its due, I open up one treatise after another that neglects the subject. The story is different when I pull out books by the great Western political and social thinkers of the past. They had no doubts about the importance of education. Plato, Rousseau, and John Dewey held very different opinions about the good life and the good society, but each knew that his vision of the ideal state depended in the last analysis on an equally bold conception of education. All three understood that without a theory of education to complement their theories of politics and society, their philosophies would be hopelessly incomplete, if not fatally flawed. Plato's *Republic* is as much a treatise on education as on politics. Rousseau, who called the *Republic* "the most beautiful educational treatise ever written,"[1] published his own educational treatise, *Emile*, the very same year as *The Social Contract*. And Dewey, a theorist of democracy par excellence, made education the centerpiece of his entire philosophy.

Nor did feminist philosophers of the past ignore the subject of education. Mary Wollstonecraft's *A Vindication of the Rights of Woman* is often read as a political, not an educational, treatise, but in fact it is both. And Wollstonecraft is not the only feminist theorist of yore to have taken education seriously. So, what has happened to change our minds about education? What's at stake here?

Playing the devil's advocate, I try to convince myself that feminist indifference to education makes no difference to women. I make no progress, but in short order list three compelling reasons why indifference is a dangerous policy.

My first reason is that the education gap keeps us from comprehending and ultimately transforming the context and conditions in which we pursue our scholarly investigations. The academy we have entered is not the pure research institution Veblen wrote about in 1906. It is an arm of that most central cultural practice of them all, education.

Second on my list of reasons is that the education gap in the feminist text prevents us from fulfilling our dreams. Whatever the long-range goals of a feminist scholar may be, the slighting of education makes them doubly difficult to achieve. As Plato needed a new theory of education for the male and female rulers of the just state he put forward in the *Republic*, feminist social and political theorists need a new, well-thought-out theory of the education of the male and female citizens and family members in the egalitarian, the just, the peace-loving societies they envision. To do without is to accept existing educational structures and assumptions unquestioningly. But these structures and assumptions are the educational correlates of an outdated gender ideology.

My third reason why the education gap is harmful to women is that it causes us to act irresponsibly toward our students and ourselves. When feminist scholars are aware that there is a whole literature on gender and education yet behave as if there is not; when we know that both educational theory and practice are genderized yet pretend otherwise; when, complacently ignoring the subject of education, we abdicate responsibility for the ends we ourselves posit: We act toward our students in what Jean Paul Sartre and other existentialist philosophers have called "bad faith."

Upon returning home from my second philosophical expedition, I asked the young Virginia, whose profile adorns the front cover of my diary, why feminist scholars seem oblivious to the sorry state of the academic terrain. Shaking her head she replied: "I told you that if women joined the procession across the bridge they would start behaving like their brothers."

Although I knew she was right, I felt sure there was more to the story. To discover what that "more" might be, I decided to make one last excursion into the academy's territory.

❯ ❯ ❯

As I shut my office door, strode down the long corridor, and stepped for my third and last time onto the academy's huge expanse, I reviewed what I, a lifelong student of education, knew about the subject. First and foremost, I knew that education turns each and every one of us from a creature of nature, so to speak, into a creature of culture: that it supplies the attitudes, values, and ideologies we carry with us into each and every encounter with the world. From my own research on gender and education begun in 1980 and continuing to this day, I also knew that just about all of us—parents, politicians, school teachers and administrators, and just plain citizens—implicitly divide social reality into Woolf's two worlds. Once having done so, we take it for granted that the function of education is to transform children who have heretofore lived their lives in the world of the private home into members of the world of work, politics, and the professions. Furthermore, assuming that the private home is a natural institution and that, accordingly, membership in it is a given rather than something one must achieve, we see no reason to prepare people to carry out the tasks and activities associated with it. In contrast, perceiving the public world as a human creation and membership in it as something at which one can succeed or fail and therefore as problematic, we make preparation for carrying out the tasks and activities associated with it the business of education.

Now none of this in itself makes education gendered. That quality is conferred by the fact that, culturally speaking, Woolf's two worlds are gendered, with the one world considered men's domain and the other women's. Gender thus becomes a basic dimension of the whole educational system: so basic, in fact, that it permeates our culture's educational ideals, aims, curricula, methodologies, and organizational structures.

Woolf said that life in the world across the bridge from the private home is competitive and that the people there have to be pugnacious and possessive in order to succeed. In our educational thought and practice, we in the West signify our agreement with her by assuming that love, nurturance, and the 3 Cs of care, concern, and connection—all qualities associated with the private home and with women—run counter to education's raison d'être. Indeed, we take these to be such obstacles to the achievement of the objective of preparing people for membership in the public world that we make one of school's main tasks that of casting off the attitudes and values, the patterns of thought and action associated with home, women, and domesticity.

The very year I began my study of women and education this scenario was played out before my eyes. During the question period at a symposium on literacy sponsored by one of this nation's most eminent schools of education, a young woman in the audience raised her hand. "The panel did not mention the research that shows that children learn best in a supportive, caring atmosphere," she said. "Would anyone be willing to comment on how this body of work relates to the teaching of adult literacy?" To my astonishment, for she had been very polite, instead of turning to the symposiasts to ask who among them would like to respond, the chair of the proceedings turned on her. "Surely you are aware that teachers are overburdened, that they already have too much to do. You cannot seriously be suggesting that faculties of education should teach teachers to be caring too," scoffed this man who had built his reputation on the advocacy of enlightened teaching methods.

Had I not witnessed his metamorphosis from a mild-mannered professor into a derisive defender of heartless schooling, I would not have believed it possible. Yet the audience in that huge auditorium gave not one sign of dismay. On the contrary, it seemed to share the moderator's belief that the young woman had violated a taboo. Only as I was writing my third report for the Society of Feminist Scholars and Their Friends did I realize that this is exactly what she had done. Assigning the 3Cs of care, concern, and connection to the world of the private home, *the education-gender system* renders these improper virtues for educators to promote and inappropriate—even forbidden—topics for them to discuss.

Why can't a woman be more like a man? An educated woman in the public arena not only can be like a man, she must be. This is what the education-gender system mandates. By speaking out about something she should have known better than to discuss openly, the young woman at the literacy conference proved herself a stranger in a strange land. How many women before and since have done likewise! How many of us have been humiliated in much the same way! Who amongst us has not taken vows of silence rather than commit the same gaffe!

Every educated woman must monitor her speech and behavior lest she do the unacceptable. None of us can ever be sure that our speech or behavior patterns will not some day betray us. And women who make the academy their home have an added burden. We are in the unenviable position of transmitting to future generations the very educational ideology that turns women into living contradictions—into people who are and are not women; or are and are not men. Like any other guild, the academy charges its members an annual fee. One portion of the admission price that men and women alike must pay is complicity in this process.

A stranger to the academy may think it odd that feminist scholars who detect the workings of gender in just about every other facet of human existence take an uncritical attitude toward education. An outsider might expect education to be a primary concern of those who are at once its prime "products" and its faithful transmitters.

One of the books I carried with me on my third philosophical expedition across the scholarly terrain was Ivan Illich's *Deschooling Society*. This small volume, published in 1972, argued that schooling perpetuates itself through a hidden curriculum that teaches dependency on schools. Confusing process and substance, school successfully transmits the lesson that to get an education you must go to school. Well, education perpetuates itself, too. I do not mean that, as educated people, we become addicted to education, although this may be true. Rather, we are indoctrinated in the belief that education has a fixed unchanging nature: so indoctrinated, indeed, that although feminist scholars insist that apparently natural phenomena like the family, the human body, and gender are actually social constructions, most of us treat education as the exception that proves the rule. Assuming that the goals and functions, definitions and boundaries of education that they took for granted when they were being educated are immutable givens, they treat these as eternal and immutable features of the academic landscape. Never dreaming that there might be alternatives, they cannot even see the possibilities that exist.

As creators of women's studies and active contributors to such other recent additions to the curriculum as African-American studies and gay and lesbian studies, feminist academics know that the subjects of the liberal curriculum do not come ready-made. We know that they are not God-given; that there are no preexisting bundles of subject matter out there just waiting to be noticed. But to understand that the subjects we and others have inserted into liberal education are human constructions is one thing. To realize that the traditional subjects of the liberal curriculum—history, philosophy, physics, and the rest—are also constructs, that both the liberal curriculum and liberal education itself are such, and that these and our other educational constructs are deeply gendered, is quite another.

Those who essentialize education rule out the very possibility of change; in their eyes, discussion of said topic appears futile. Why talk about what is part of a thing's very nature and therefore cannot be altered? Why try to formulate a new vision of education when the old one—in its broad outlines, if not its minute details—is the only conceivable one?

Still, there is more at stake in the education gap than simply a misplaced essentialism. I have already mentioned the academy's acceptance of the principle of guilt by association. A person does not have to spend much time in the academy to discover that the study of education is considered so demeaning that to be a scholar who specializes in education is to live in a permanent state of embarrassment. I speak from experience. My self-confidence knows no bounds when someone asks what my field is, for I am well aware that philosophy is considered a weighty subject. When, however, I am questioned about my specialty within philosophy, I experience acute discomfort. Do I declare my allegiance to philosophy of education or trade on my secondary interest in the philosophy of science? To opt for the latter course of action is to deny a central aspect of my identity. To choose the former is to advertise my own insignificance. I have seen scholars faced with this same dilemma reiterate that they are in philosophy—or sociology, psychology, history, as the case may be—and then change the subject. I have known others who have simply refused to describe their research. And over the years I have watched those who started out in philosophy—or sociology, psychology, history—of education shift their research interests onto safer ground.

The reason for the hedgings and avoidances is not difficult to discern. It does your standing as an academic no good whatsoever for it to become known that you specialize in education. The academy's devaluation of the social institution and practice of education is incontrovertible. According to its policy of guilt by association, a discipline has only as much status as its objects of study, and each scholar has only as much status as his or her discipline. As it happens, the academy's devaluation of education—I should really say of early childhood education and schooling since it does value itself—is matched by its treatment of home economics and nursing. View the academy's ratings of these three fields as independent, isolated events and one sees three separate areas of questionable academic repute. Look at the three together, and one perceives that old double standard at work.

Feminist scholars who originally flagged the trap of the double standard had in mind the academy's practice of ranking men's lives, works, and deeds far above women's. Where are Austen, Eliot, and the Brontës, they asked. What have you done with Emily Dickinson, Elizabeth Barrett Browning, Virginia Woolf, and Zora Neale Hurston? They did not add—perhaps they did not then notice—that the trap also applies to the subjects of the academy's curriculum and the research interests of its faculty. Yet the academy values those subjects of study and objects of inquiry that are culturally associated with men far above the ones associated with women. When one thinks of the education-gender system, the unequal valuations make sense. Why are the fields of education, nursing, homemaking so scorned by the academy, so deprecated that they are usually considered to fall beyond the very borders of liberal learning? Their objects of study and inquiry—teaching, nursing, homemaking— are historically associated with home and family. Considered women's domains, these areas are tainted in the academy's eyes by the second-class citizenship of the people who practice them. Even more telling, the historical association of these practices with the world of the private home sullies them.

A stranger to the academy might suppose that feminist scholars would have a heightened awareness of this application of the double standard. She or he might think that we, at least, would know how harmful it is to value men more than women, the public world more than the private; and would have gone out of our ways to avoid it. Yet our harsh treatment of Gilligan and so many other women bears mute testimony to our capacity to be just as influenced by the academy's hidden messages as our nonfeminist colleagues, and a double standard regarding topics worthy of study and inquiry is one of the main lessons transmitted by that implicit curriculum.

That our attitude toward home—a.k.a. female—associated topics of inquiry has changed as we have become ensconced in the academy is another sign that our behavior is far more governed by the double standard than we realize. In the 1970s and early 1980s, women and gender, mothering and the family were among our first and favorite topics of inquiry. As our hopes of belonging increased, cries of essentialism filled the air, and these same items began turning up on our lists of proscribed categories. Did male-associated topics such as justice, power, science, democracy, the economy also grace our lists? As if to confirm the existence of an education-gender system, male-associated categories gained our favor even as female-associated ones were outlawed. The criticisms made of the one set of topics could just as well have been directed at the other, but in a glaring application of the double standard they were not.

One obvious consequence of the academy's denigration of education, nursing, homemaking, and the other activities, institutions, and personal qualities that have culturally and historically been associated with women and the home is the perpetuation of the devaluation of those phenomena by the world at large. Equally pernicious, when feminist scholars fall into the trap of the double standard, the academy's denigration of what it sees as "Other" is transmuted into a form of self-hatred. For the truth is that the occupations which were historically practiced mainly by women to a great extent still are.

The academy likes to think of itself as an independent, autonomous realm sealed off from the outside world. It takes pleasure in imagining itself as the upholder of intellectual values and the opponent of cultural prejudices. Scholars who have shown the extent to which status in the academy mirrors that in the outside world know better. Yet although they enthusiastically document the presence inside the academy of some of the outside world's invidious comparisons, they ignore those in which gender is implicated.

In repeating the culture's attitudes toward girls and women and also toward the institutions, activities, occupations, and other items it associates with them, the academy reinforces the denigration. On the one hand, women's devaluation of home- and female-associated objects of study and inquiry constitutes a kind of self-denigration. Yet she who values them runs the risk of being denigrated by everyone else. And as if this were not bad enough, she who would resist the double standard must allay feminist fears that an interest in girls, women, and assorted female-associated phenomena will imprison us once again in the kitchens and nurseries from whence we sprang.

> > >

In retrospect it is easy to see that many of the sightings of feminist scholars in and around the traps of essentialism and false generalization were motivated by an intense fear of "refeminization"—of women's falling or being pushed back into conformity to the old gender roles and relationships. The time is past when women can be deported from the world of work, politics, and the professions to the one from whence we came. The two-parent family in which Father goes out to work and Mother stays home is no longer the norm. Besides, our participation in the land of paid work, politics, and the professions has become well nigh essential to men, women, and children. Nonetheless, the old female occupations persist in new forms.

Indeed, the process of relocating us into fields of work that represent the equivalents of activities that were once housed in the traditional home is well under way, if not already completed.

Woolf did not tell us that the world across the bridge is built on a hillside. She did not say that the doors opening into law, medicine, politics, engineering, banking, investment, and the other male bastions of her day are situated on the heights and that the climb is steep. Nor did she tell us that across the bridge two roads diverge. She did not say that the "choice" for educated women would be between walking up to the historically male professions on the heights or down to the historically female ones. Who knows? She may not have foreseen that women's options would consist of two kinds of paid professions: one high and the other low, one valued and the other denigrated. She may not have anticipated that the great majority of women would pick the "female" ones.

Call the gender tracking in the workplace what you will. Call it free choice, ghettoization, the refeminization of women. The worst fear of many feminists—namely, that the late-twentieth century's liberated women might end up repeating an earlier female existence—has come to pass.

Is the reality of women's continuing to perform what was traditionally considered to be women's work something to be deplored? Let me say here and now that a number of the activities and processes that the culture has traditionally assigned to women in the private home are as important to the well being of society and its members as any could possibly be. I deplore their devaluation, not their presence in the public world. I also deplore the grossly unequal distribution of men and women in those occupations now called "the caring professions." The tracking of women into them is troubling in part because these are also low-paying, low-status occupations. Even more important, it is a dangerous policy to divide up society's work between the sexes in such a way that the 3Cs of care, concern, and connection continue to be women's responsibility when what is so desperately needed is that they become women's *and* men's.

But the process of women's refeminization goes beyond the gender tracking in the workplace. As long ago as 1984 a feminist author wrote, "we are currently witnessing a renewed interest in femininity and an unabashed indulgence in feminine pursuits."[2] In 1990 researchers reported that undergraduate women were baking cookies for their boyfriends and washing their clothes.[3] At Harvard University, where in 1996 I was a visiting professor of education, an undergraduate woman told my class that all but two of her women friends had experienced eating disorders while in college. She also said that despite the young women's obvious academic talents—or possibly because of them—the main question on their minds was their ability to attract male partners in both the short and the long run.

Do the facts of refeminization vindicate the accusations of essentialism, the disdain for occupations traditionally viewed as women's, and the avoidance of female-associated research topics? No, the accusatory research climate stifles feminist inquiry while dividing us from each other; the policy of banning female-associated categories like women and mothering limits the illumination our research can provide; and the education gap in our text keeps us from comprehending the circumstances of our employment. The more general policy of shunning female-associated objects of research is not justified either.

As many feminists have pointed out, the uncritical valorizing or romanticizing or sentimentalizing of what have historically been considered women's values, skills, attitudes, and ways of life is a perilous policy. At best it ends up glorifying domestic abuse and abandonment, poverty, exhaustion, resentment, and that oft-celebrated commodity—female self-sacrifice. At worst, it causes our daughters, if not ourselves, to embrace the old oppressive roles, expectations, and behavior patterns. Yet if the sentimentality trap is best avoided, it is as stifling and intimidating to attach the uncritical valorization or romanticizing labels automatically to every bit of research that casts female-associated phenomena in a positive light as it is to apply the essentialist label indiscriminately. Surely, a feminist scholar can investigate female culturally associated phenomena without romanticizing them. She can also do so without wallowing in her own victimization.

Contrasting "victim feminism" and "power feminism," Naomi Wolf correctly said that a victim identity is likely "to entrench people in apathy and despair, thus keeping them from trying to change their victim status."[4] Still, it does women no good at all to deny our domination, mistreatment, and oppression throughout history and across cultures. As Audre Lorde said in *Sister Outsider*, "One tool of the Great-American-Double-Think is to blame the victim for victimization."[5] One of the great contributions of those consciousness-raising groups that sprang up in the late 1960s and early 1970s was to persuade women that we are not always to blame for what has happened to us. One of the most important achievements of the feminist scholarship of the 1970s—I am thinking, for instance, of Susan Brownmiller's *Against Our Will*, Barbara Ehrenreich and Deirdre English's *For Her Own Good*, Ann Oakley's *Woman's Work*, Adrienne Rich's *Of Woman Born*, Cellestine Ware's *Woman Power*—was to teach women that, where our own oppression by sex or sex plus race is concerned, the fault lies in society, not ourselves.

Sentimentality and victimization are the two sides of a coin. She who falls into the sentimentality trap may end up perpetuating phenomena that historically were oppressive to women by making them attractive to her daughters. She who celebrates her victimization risks keeping it alive by projecting it into her future. Just as a scholar who romanticizes female-associated institutions, practices, and the like is apt to do more harm than good by her very choice of research topic, so too is one who dwells on how pitiable are the victims of said phenomena.

Yet silence has its own dangers. George Santayana is the one who worried that those who do not remember the past are condemned to repeat it. It is naive to think that the truth alone will set one free. Much, much more than truth is needed to combat oppression and victimization. But to be like Pollyanna, the good girl of storybook fame, and play the "glad game" of refusing to think about past suffering and choosing instead to look only on the bright side of things is likely to preclude the very possibility of that "more."

Philosopher Sandra Bartky once characterized a feminist consciousness as "consciousness of victimization."[6] Adding that this consciousness is a profoundly divided awareness, she wrote:

> To see myself as victim is to know that I have already sustained injury, that I live exposed to injury, that I have been at worst mutilated, at best diminished in my being. But at the same time, feminist consciousness is a joyous consciousness of one's own power, of the possibility of unprecedented personal growth and the release of energy long suppressed.[7]

In hiding the harsh realities of women's collective past from ourselves and others, those who fall into the Pollyanna trap of suppressing the unpleasantness deprive one and all of just that understanding, which is needed if the world is ever to become a more hospitable place for women.

Why do so few feminist scholars consider the study of education to be a serious intellectual endeavor? Why is it so hard for academic feminists not only to give education its due but to do *any* female-associated research topic scholarly justice? Add up the new gender tracking, the best-selling book, the preoccupation with body image among some of this nation's most brilliant women undergraduates, and what does one get? The sum total I keep reaching is that the worst fear of feminist scholars—women's refeminization—is being enacted.

Yes, things have changed. When I graduated from college in 1951, the employment office presented three options to those of us who were not yet engaged to be married. No matter that my roommate was about to enter medical school. No matter that two or three women of my class were planning to attend law school. The rest of us could expect to become secretaries, librarians, or social workers before settling down as full-time wives and mothers. Commerce, banking, engineering, politics, journalism, the ministry, the higher learning, and all the other traditionally male fields now open to women were in my day considered beyond the pale. Then again: when in the late 1960s I found myself practicing one of those men's professions, the two male graduate students assigned to be teaching fellows in my philosophy of education course refused the job saying outright that they would not work for a woman.

I cannot imagine this happening today. Yet although the changes are enormous and very real, they neither cancel out our refeminization nor eradicate the self-defeating consequences of our fear. Granted, there are many reasons besides a fear of refeminization why those who wish to be full-fledged members of the academy might eschew female-associated research topics. But insofar as that fear causes a feminist scholar to turn her back on the study of girls, women, gender, and related topics, she forswears the very research that could rescue women in this time of need. Spurning the knowledge that might have helped stem the tide of our refeminization, she denies her mothers, daughters, sisters, half-sisters, female cousins, and aunts the possibility of coming to understand why it is proceeding apace, what forms it is taking, what harm it is doing women, and how it might be combated.

In an age when knowledge has been shown to be implicated in the subordination and oppression of women and other groups, it is hardly surprising that our optimism about its liberatory tendencies is not what it was in the 1970s. Still, it is a far cry from our earlier assumption that knowledge can be power to the magical thinking of those who now walk into the Pollyanna trap of suppressing the unpleasantness. Feminist scholars are the last people one would expect to find caught in this pitfall. Yet there we are, our fear of refeminization having fueled our Pollyanna-like belief that what you do not talk about will not return to haunt you.

In Eleanor Porter's book *Pollyanna,* the glad game transforms society. Although poverty is not erased and illness not eradicated, everyone is content. Would that every person could attain happiness by this simple remedy! Better still, would that the glad game could tear out women's refeminization by its very roots. But even Pollyanna knew that the game offered its players no such prizes.

One lesson to be learned from the replication within the world of work, politics, and the professions of the gendered division of labor that used to span Woolf's two worlds is that society has a crying need for the occupations and practices that tradition placed in women's charge. Another is that without a concerted effort to change the cultural assumption that girls and women are carers by nature and that boys and men are not, either women will do the major portion of society's so-called caring work or it will not be done.

I have sometimes heard it said that Gilligan's discovery of the different voice—a voice that gives expression to the ethic of care—is responsible for the expectation that girls and women will continue to do the major part of society's emotional labor. Although this is a particularly egregious example of women's self-blame, those feminist scholars who have warned that research on girls, women, and other female-associated phenomena are likely to be held against us do have a point. To highlight our vulnerability is not and never was a mistake. The mistake has been to reject research that sheds light on ourselves and to walk away from the admittedly difficult problem of discovering how to change the culture's gendered expectations and division of all forms of labor.

And now, as if reflecting the shape of my three expeditions, my argument comes full circle, for education is implicated in both the fact of our refeminization and the prospect of turning the tide. This means that we have got to close the education gap in the feminist text. Otherwise, even if feminist scholars undertake the desperately needed project of discovering how to undo the refeminization, their proposals for action will almost certainly be wanting.

Rendering the education-gender system invisible, the education gap fosters the illusion that fundamental social reform—which is what gender equality in the workplace and the refusal to conform to the old female stereotype are—can be achieved without also undertaking fundamental educational reform. It also perpetuates the myth that whatever changes in education feminist scholars might think necessary can be accomplished by simply inserting what is wanted into the existing system. Above all the education gap hides from us the fact that because our education system is thoroughly gendered, in order to effect the desired changes in society, the system itself must be dismantled.

> > >

What price belonging? Can feminist scholars find acceptance in the academy without losing sight of our mothers, daughters, sisters, half-sisters, female cousins, and aunts? Can we find it without becoming divided from our past, present, and future selves?

The evidence accumulates. On my first philosophical expedition into the academic workplace I witnessed our separation from each other. On my second field trip I saw us detaching ourselves from women outside the academy—from feminist activists and from all the other women in the world. Then, on my third and last journey, I watched feminist scholars:

> turn away from women-related teaching subjects and research topics—in the name of anti-sentimentality and victimization;

> and turn their backs on the traditional female professions and their practitioners—for fear of refeminization.

These in a nutshell were my findings. Compare them with the high hopes of feminist scholars in the 1970s and one can only conclude that in search of acceptance in the academy, we have let go of our dreams. Yet it would be a terrible mistake to place the blame on feminist scholars and to leave it at that. Is not the academy the one responsible for cutting us off from our activist roots and estranging us from women? Is not the price of admission it charges women far too steep?

An Immigrant Interpretation

PART TWO

CHAPTER 1
WOMEN AS IMMIGRANTS

The year feminist scholars began heralding our acceptance by the academy was also the year we began saying that feminist scholarship had attained its maturity.[1] Yet the parallels between our collective estrangement and the dissociation of the adolescent girls Gilligan has studied are striking.

"Adolescence seems a watershed in female development, a time when girls are in danger of drowning or disappearing," Gilligan wrote in 1990.[2] When the preadolescent girls she and her colleagues were studying visited the Boston Museum of Fine Arts they spoke plainly and irreverently. Asked how girls and women appear in the museum, one unhesitatingly said "naked."[3] Discussing a painting of "Reverend John Atwood and His Family," another concluded that the wife "looks very worn and tired."[4] Then things changed. When interviewed at age 12, one of the girls used the phrase "I don't know" twenty-one times. At age 13, with no corresponding increase in the length of her interview transcript, the phrase appeared sixty-seven times. By age 14 the tally was 135. In one study a girl who was approaching adolescence told about "losing confidence in myself. I was losing track of myself, really, and losing the kind of person I was."[5]

Gilligan and her colleagues witnessed "the onset of dissociative processes"[6] in girls at adolescence. When girls do not say what is on their minds and in their hearts they are in danger of losing touch with themselves, yet they hide what they know and what they feel for the sake of their relationships to others. "It seems easier, in many ways, for girls to cover their experience and not know what they know," says Gilligan, "and because this covering coincides with the historical covering of women's and girls' experiences and voices, it is easily dissociated, set apart from consciousness, forgotten."[7]

What Gilligan saw happen to girls at adolescence I have seen happen to feminist scholars in the academy. When I read that at the edge of adolescence girls begin to feel "the mesmerizing presence of the perfect girl" and that with her arrival "girls are in danger of losing their world,"[8] I think of feminist academics' own quest for perfection. I think of

> how much more harshly we have come to judge women's work than men's;

> how much more likely we are to accuse women scholars of racism, classism, and heterosexism;

> how much more determined we are to purge our own theories of allegedly essentialist and ahistorical categories than those of men,

and I realize that in our pursuit of the ideal of the perfect woman we have taken to self-flagellation.

When I find out that girls at adolescence are encouraged to disconnect themselves from their bodies,[9] I think of our attempts at disconnection. I think of

> the education gap in our text,

> the aerial distance we put between ourselves and the harsh realities of women's lived experience,

> and the esoteric language that creates a wall between feminist theorists and feminist activists,

and I appreciate how skillful feminist scholarship has become in distancing itself from embodied women.

When I hear how reluctant to back down 11- and 12-year-old girls are when asked, "Are you sure?"[10] and then learn how unsure of themselves they become, I think of how difficult it has become for us to speak plainly and irreverently. I think of

> the commentator on Gilligan's research on girls who after judging this work to ring "personally, disturbingly true" and to contain "impressively fruitful insights" advised her to abandon the project;[11]

> the endless qualifications inserted in our own writings that effectively obscure our meaning;

> and the countless lectures bearing the words "from a feminist perspective" in their titles that discuss race or class or both and say little or nothing about women or gender,

and I conclude that we have lost the ability we once had to speak our minds.

The research done by Gilligan and her colleagues shows that "for girls coming of age in this culture at this time, adolescence marks a potential point of departure from life experience."[12] For feminist theorists and researchers collectively, coming of age in this academy has marked the same point of departure. Wanting to be in relationship with the academy and aware of the political consequences of speaking our minds and hearts, we have become estranged from the knowledge we acquired when we first began doing research on women and from the anger and amazement, passion and determination that our discoveries called forth.

Our estrangement from women is the social counterpart of adolescent girls' psychological dissociation. It is not a conscious maneuver. Nobody said: Let us forget what we found out about ourselves and the world. No one told us to stop being whistle blowers. As with adolescent girls, our collective dissociation is an adaptive response to the extraordinarily difficult situation in which we find ourselves.

The collective estrangement of feminist scholars from our roots also bears an uncanny resemblance to that of immigrant groups in the United States in the nineteenth and early twentieth centuries. Near the end of a landmark study of immigration in American life, sociologist Milton Gordon asked some pointed questions:

> › What are the consequences for the several major ethnic subsocieties in America of the fact that many, perhaps a large majority, of the most intellectually inclined of their birthright members are siphoned off, as it were . . . retaining only a minimal concern, if any, for the communal life and issues of their parental group?

> › Does the outflow of intellectuals . . . their subsequent estrangement from the life of these groups, and the resultant block in communication between the ethnic subsociety and the intellectual have dysfunctional consequences?

> › Do the major decisions both in the society as a whole and within the ethnic subsociety come to be made with the intellectual excluded from the decision-making process?

> › Do the intellectuals themselves lose out in breadth and vision as a result of this estrangement?[13]

These are the selfsame questions I am asking about academic feminists. Gordon wanted to know if the siphoning off of immigrant intellectuals is inevitable "in the very nature of things."[14] I do not for a moment believe that the estrangement of feminist scholars from our mothers, daughters, sisters, halfsisters, female cousins, and aunts, which amounts to a betrayal of our intentions and a maiming of ourselves, is inevitable. The immigrant analogy is helpful here, for even as it highlights the "naturalness" of our estrangement, it holds open the possibility of reconnection.

In 1911, a woman named Mary Antin wrote an autobiography called *The Promised Land*. I summon up her imagery to mark the big difference between the men in Virginia Woolf's procession across the bridge connecting the two worlds and the women I see today. Those men were not foreigners in the world of politics, work, and the professions. We women are. The land we immigrants walk into has long belonged to men. It has been ours only in our dreams.

In his groundbreaking history, *The Uprooted*, historian Oscar Handlin called the story of nineteenth-century immigration to the United States "a history of alienation and its consequences."[15] Emigration took people "out of traditional, accustomed environments and replanted them in strange ground, among strangers, where strange manners prevailed."[16] As I write, the plight of women in my own country and many other nations resonates with Antin's first-person and Handlin's third-person renditions of the immigrant experience. Indeed, so well do the commentaries of Handlin and Antin elucidate women's entrance into the world of work, politics, and the professions that I offer forthwith an immigrant interpretation of that world historic event.

Antin reported that after her family arrived in America in the late-nineteenth century, the children "were let loose on the street."[17] In all branches of domestic education "chaos took the place of system; uncertainty, inconstancy undermined discipline."[18] Making it clear that parents had become unmoored from the rites and rituals, customs and habits in which they had been trained, she wrote, "In public deportment, in etiquette, in all matters of social intercourse, they had no standards to go by, seeing that America was not Polotzk."[19]

With customary modes of behavior inadequate and with old ties broken, said Handlin, the immigrants "faced the enormous compulsion of working out new relationships, new meanings to their lives, often under harsh and hostile circumstances."[20] And because "emigration had stripped away the veneer that in more stable situations concealed the underlying nature of the social structure,"[21] the responses could not be easy or automatic. On the contrary, "every act was crucial, the product of conscious weighing of alternatives, never simple conformity to an habitual pattern."[22]

For those women who have entered professions like university teaching, medicine, the clergy, law, banking, and commerce, the smallest actions—even walking and talking, eating and dressing, smiling and scowling—are objects of conscious decision-making. Should I wear my hair long or short? an attorney asks herself. Do I put on pants or a skirt to give this lecture? a professor wonders aloud. On the plane home from a conference in Sweden, I read a newspaper article chastising businesswomen for wearing running shoes rather than high heels on their lunch breaks.

With customary modes of behavior inadequate, with no new rules in place for women's new roles and environments, and with men frequently at a loss as to how to act in women's presence, there is also an enormous compulsion to work out new relationships.

> In a television documentary about her work, Melissa Franklin, the first woman to be granted tenure in Harvard University's physics department, says that she plans to tell the next male colleague who calls her a hysterical female: "Knock it off. Learn how to interact with me as your equal."

> A female student in a physical science program at a British polytechnic institute reports:
> "When we first met the lads, they wouldn't swear or anything, they were really nice; and then, after about two or three weeks, they realized that you weren't any different to them and just went back to normal, but the first weeks were really strange because they were so nice it was unbelievable, and you wondered what you were doing, they'd hold open the door, they wouldn't swear, if they swore they'd apologize."[23]

> Six male students at the Harvard Business School were disciplined in April 1998 for having spent an entire year harassing their female classmates. "Harvard Business School really

condones an atmosphere of boot camp, a sort of 'frat boy' atmosphere," one school alumna told a reporter.[24]

> Then there is the psychological and verbal abuse reported to a U.S. Senate Committee by the woman in line to be the next chief of police in Springfield, Massachusetts:

A sanitary napkin was taped to one female officer's locker, an artificial penis was put in another's desk drawer; sexually demeaning cartoons, with female officers' names scrawled on the characters, were posted in common areas; one male officer told a female officer he wanted to dress her in a Girl Scout uniform and rape her.[25]

> There is also the experience of a woman sports writer in the locker room of the New England Patriots football team:

The incident was initiated by a player who walked over to Olson and thrust his penis toward her asking, "Do you want to take a bite out of this?" It escalated quickly as several more players paraded past her, "modeling" their genitals in a mock strip tease while various others shouted: "Did she look, did she look?" "Get her to look"; "That's what she wants"; "Is she looking," "Make her look."[26]

> And there is the shocking testimony that on Wall Street male coworkers, supervisors, and owners of firms grab women's breasts, buttocks, and genitals; call women unprintable names; and threaten to get women fired if they do not provide sexual favors.[27]

Virginia Woolf had no illusions about that world on the other side of the bridge. But although she wanted women to think twice before entering men's world, she did not mention its assimilationist policies. She did not tell us how loath this land was to receive newcomers. She neglected to say that only those brave souls who could demonstrate their ability to think and act like the natives would be able to establish residency there. Nor did Woolf inform us that the task of assimilating foreigners had been given over to education.

Woolf's image of the procession diverts attention from these vital issues. Her metaphor of a bridge connecting the world of the private home to the world of work, politics, and the professions begs the big educational questions for both women and men. In placing men on the bridge who have already been educated, she effectively excludes from the discussion education's culturally designated function of preparing people for life in the world of paid work, politics, and the professions. When Woolf asks if women should join the procession of educated men, the implication is that the objectionable traits we would acquire upon becoming doctors, lawyers, and the rest are by-products of the professions themselves. But the education-gender system insures that education is not a neutral spectator in the transformational process.

According to Handlin:

> The immigrants lived in crisis because they were uprooted. In transplantation, while the old roots were sundered, before the new were established, the immigrants existed in an extreme situation. The shock, and the effects of the shock, persisted for many years; and their influence reached down to generations which themselves never paid the cost of crossing.[28]

Untold numbers of women—among them the feminist scholars in the academy—now live in crisis because the roots of the old gendered divisions of labor have been sundered. And while one might have expected education to alleviate the shock and its effects, it has proved itself to be in the service of quite a different end.

"The crossing in all its phases was a harsh and brutal filter," wrote Handlin. "On land in Europe, in the port of embarkation, on the ocean, in the port of arrival, and on land in America, it introduced a decisive range of selective factors that operated to let through only a few of those who left the Old World."[29] Some of the selective factors were physical. The trek across Europe could cover as much as 300 miles, and hunger, illness, assaults by beasts and humans were common occurrences.[30] Other factors had to do with an individual's ability to adapt, for "only those who were capable of adjusting from peasant ways to the needs of new conditions and new challenges were able to absorb the successive shocks of migration."[31]

To find a harsh and brutal filter that lets relatively few women into the Promised Land unscathed we need look no further than that thing called education. Education is by no means the only filter of girls and women. Family, church, peer groups, and media all do their part. But the existence of other screening devices does not diminish education's central role in maintaining the "purity" of the Promised Land. That women scholars, whether feminist or not, stand in a special relationship to education by virtue of our membership in the academy does not negate its filtering function, either. For us the academy is both filter and chosen destination. As Antin's family settled in the Boston area of their Promised Land, we seek to establish ourselves in the academic sector of the world of paid work, politics, and the professions.

CHAPTER 11

THE NEW
GENDER TRACKING

Divide education into consecutive phases as Handlin did the crossing and it is easy to see that in elementary schools, secondary schools, undergraduate colleges, graduate and professional schools, and the professions themselves, selective factors now operate on women. At the elementary and secondary levels these include the well-documented chilly coeducational classroom climate for girls, the equally well-documented if far more shocking sexual harassment of girls by boys, and the relative lack of curriculum content about girls and women. Lest it be thought that "lower" education is a party to the filtering process whereas higher education is just an innocent bystander, bear in mind the statistics from Sweden, a country that has for decades been committed to a policy of gender equality. At last count, approximately 65 percent of Sweden's undergraduates were female, 60 percent of those receiving undergraduate degrees were female, 40 percent of those entering what they call the postgraduate level and what we in the U.S. would label graduate-level studies were female, and 28 percent of Ph.D. recipients were female.[1]

One hears this same story of attrition wherever one goes.[2] And one need but glance around to detect signs of a new tracking system in the halls of academe.

In 1982, members of the faculty of Lewis and Clark, a coeducational college in Oregon whose official policy has always been to offer the same curriculum to both sexes, became concerned that male and female students were choosing different courses and electing different majors. In 1867, men and women had pursued the same course of study—except for mathematics, which women were not required to take. One-hundred-fifteen years and at least two women's movements later it was something of a surprise, therefore, to discover that things had changed. After the college adopted the presumably progressive policy of curricular electives, the men ended up congregating in the natural and physical sciences, business, political science, and economics. The women meanwhile gravitated to the humanities, psychology, sociology, and biology, which at Lewis and Clark was weighted in favor of environmental studies.

In 1986 a similar and equally unexpected gender tracking was reported on a global level by the Organization for Economic Cooperation and Development. Indeed, even in those countries in which women made up at least half of all students, fields of study proved to be sharply divided according to sex, with women tending to predominate in those "soft" areas having low academic standing and reduced job opportunities.[3] That same year the National Research Council in the U.S. reported that whereas the majority of doctoral recipients in English and American languages and literatures and in foreign languages and literatures were women, men represented about seven-eighths of new Ph.D.s in engineering and the mathematical and physical sciences.[4]

Standing one day in the 1990s on one of those crowded buses that shuttles people from their places of work back to their private homes each evening, I overheard two men in business attire marvel at the fact that almost all the women they knew had majored in language or literature as undergraduates. "They chose to do it, you know, and look where they are now," said the one. "Secretaries and paralegals," replied the other.

It is customary to use the language of "choice" when discussing higher education's gendered division of study. Insofar as college and university students elect their courses from a wide range of alternatives, this terminology may accurately reflect the facts, yet it is deeply deceptive. "Choice" rhetoric masks the degree to which the self-selection that directs girls and boys, women and men into different courses of study and, ultimately, into different occupations is influenced by social pressures, cultural expectations, and the operations of the academy's education-gender system. The terminology also diverts attention from the new version of the old gender tracking.

Historically, coeducation was viewed as a remedy for the existing two-track gender-based educational system that required girls and boys, men and women to attend separate institutions where they studied different curricula designed to fit them for their different societal roles and responsibilities. If women as well as men are to be rulers of the Just State, said Plato in the *Republic*—and it was his opinion that they should be—then they must be educated alongside the men. If the rights of men are to be extended to women, wrote Mary Wollstonecraft some 2000 years later in *A Vindication of the Rights of Woman*—and it was her conviction that they must be—then girls and boys, men and women should be educated together.

Although the project of extending men's education to women took more than two millennia to accomplish, the U.S. chapter of the story is simply told. Harvard College was founded in 1636, yet in 1776 we discover Abigail Adams writing her husband John:

> If you complain of neglect of Education in sons, What shall I say with regard to daughters . . . I most sincerely wish that some more liberal plan might be laid and executed for the Benefit of the rising Generation, and that our new constitution may be

distinguished for learning and Virtue. If we mean to have Heroes, statesmen, and Philosophers, we should have learned women.[5]

Oberlin College, which admitted women in 1833, is generally credited with being the first coeducational institution of higher learning in the U.S. This, despite the fact that the college basically offered separate curricula for men and women. Moreover, this landmark school in the history of women's education required its women students to make the men's beds and clean and cook for them, presumably in order to keep down the cost of the men's tuition.[6]

With the rise of state universities in the second half of the nineteenth century, coeducation gradually spread. Meanwhile, the establishment in that same period of the so-called "coordinate" women's colleges—Radcliffe, Pembroke, Barnard, among them—offered "the second sex" a Harvard or Brown or Columbia education in a separate institutional setting. Nevertheless, it was not until 1990 that Princeton University could advertise a series of symposia on gender and education "Commemorating 20 Years of Undergraduate Coeducation at Princeton."

Forgetting that in the U.S. the project of opening the doors of institutions of higher learning to women took almost 350 years to complete and that in older nations it took that much longer, a feminist scholar wrote in 1996: "Because most of us come from upper- or middle-class families, as soon as schools let us in we came."[7] To treat women's entrance into higher education's student body and the establishment of coeducation as the foregone conclusions of class privilege does a grave injustice to the many women and men who devoted their lives to these causes. It also misrepresents the backgrounds of the newly educated women, many of whom were very poor. Worse still, a lack of historical perspective on the time it took for institutions of higher education to open their doors to women can foster false expectations about women's other entrances into higher education—in particular, into the professoriate and into the very subject matter of the curriculum. And the myopia also precludes comparisons between the hopes and intentions of coeducation's original sponsors and the realities of the achievement.

Still, although coeducation was centuries in the making, there is no denying that by the start of the twenty-first century the condition that Plato envisioned for his utopia and that Wollstonecraft dreamed of for her daughters is an accepted way of life for millions and millions of people around the world. The trouble is that this great historical development has turned out to be a carrier of old inequities and the creator of new problems for women. No one expected that when the then-official tracking system of separate schools with distinctive curricula for males and females became all but extinct, a de facto gender-tracking system within coeducation would develop to take its place. But one has. In effect, coeducational environments have themselves become sorting devices that perform a function for the larger society very like the one that the formal mechanism of separate-sex institutions once did.

From the standpoint of those women who head for the Promised Land's low-lying areas after crossing Woolf's bridge, the "female" occupations may well represent safety zones—places within the world of paid work, politics, and the professions where women do not have to shed their gender identities. For when higher education functions as a harsh and brutal filter of women, it does so in relation to its ostensible business of turning us into good citizens of the Promised Land.

In what position does this put women? Whether we pursue a liberal, vocational, technical, or professional education, or all of the above, the presumption is that we will acquire the knowledge, skills, traits, attitudes, values, and worldviews that are considered appropriate in the world of work, politics, and the professions. As was the case for the European peasants who immigrated to the U.S. in the nineteenth century, these goods run counter to the old cultural norms as well as to our socialization by home, church, and media. But women face the added difficulty that the qualities we must strive to acquire are genderized in favor of males. By this I mean that they are valued when they are possessed by boys and men but are viewed negatively when we acquire them. Think of the rationality, the logical acumen, and the cool judgment that a liberal education aims to instill in students. Think of the emotional distance from the people whose problems are yours to solve that a professional or technical education tries to foster. These traits are thought to become a man but not a woman. The result is that in the very act of making the qualities we have to acquire our own, our status as women is cast in doubt.[8]

It is not easy day in and day out to be an aberration, a freak of culture or of nature. The psychic costs of being and not being a woman at one and the same time—or, alternatively, of not being and being a man—are enormous and the threat of ridicule is ever present. "Just an old bag who'd been hanging around Cold Spring Harbor for years" is what a famous biologist called Nobel scientist Barbara McClintock.[9] "Brown is a first-rate violinist. And just like Olympic gold medalist Florence Griffith-Joyner, the strikingly lovely Brown is a woman who knows one can be both a champion in your field and triumphantly feminine. In the first half of the concert, she wore an elegant dark formal gown. In the second half for the concerto, she wore a springtime dress of dazzling white" is how a music critic described the director of a renowned British ensemble touring American concert halls.[10]

Surely, in the eyes of many a woman a lack of status, power, and financial rewards is a small price to pay to escape the toll that the traditional "men's" occupations impose on living contradictions. Yet if from one point of view the gender tracking in the workplace appears to provide asylum, from the standpoint of an interpretation of women as immigrants, it ghettoizes women. Indeed, just as immigrants to U.S. cities crowded together in tenement neighborhoods, women can now be said to do so in devalued areas of study and work.

Handlin depicted the ghettos as places in which the immigrants could adjust to their new environment. No doubt the new ghetto dwellers are learning to adjust, but adjustment means different things in different contexts, and in the case of women's ghettoization it means second-class citizenship. "Repetition" is a keyword here. The processes and activities of women's old world—the private home—are repeated in the new one. And that is not all. Although these would not have been transplanted into the world of paid work, politics, and the professions if they had not been needed there, they are as devalued in their new location as they were in their old.

Call the gender tracking in the workplace ghettoization, free choice, the refeminization of women. Whatever the label, the harsh and brutal filter known as higher education is implicated in the process. Our education-gender system is not something fixed or static. As the world changes, so does it. The original mechanism accompanying the system's two-sphere analysis of society and its definition of education as preparation for the public sphere was a gendered division of educational labor. The assumption was that whatever training women might need in order to carry out the tasks *of* the private home would be acquired *in* the private home. While her brothers were in school, a girl would learn at her mother's knee to keep house, raise children, tend the sick and elderly, and keep her husband content. Then, in mid-nineteenth-century U.S., schools for girls were established with the professed aim of making the performance of home's tasks more efficient. Now a division between two kinds of schools—those for girls and those for boys—replaced the earlier division of labor between home and school. Next, coeducation burst on the scene. This time the education-gender system adapted by substituting for the gender-based division of schooling an Oberlin-like gender-based division of currricula within schools. And when this two-track model of coeducation was abandoned for the model of a single curriculum with electives, the unofficial gender tracking we have today emerged.

The mechanisms that support the education-gender system's two-world analysis adapt to changing conditions and so does the analysis itself. The chilly classroom climate, the absence of a genuine co-professoriate, the lack of a true cocurriculum, these and higher education's other filtering devices are not expected to feed men and women into two separate worlds. With occupations like teaching, nursing, child care, and tending the elderly, which were once performed at home and having become well established in the world of work, politics, and the professions, our ever adaptable education-gender system now divides the public world into two separate sectors. The one sector consists of what used to be considered men's occupations and the other of occupations traditionally located in the private home. The one requires traits and skills culturally associated with males, and the other demands ones culturally associated with females. The one's status is perceived to be high and the other low. The one is populated mainly by men and the other by women.

CHAPTER III
HIGHER
EDUCATION
AS FILTER

The Promised Land requires a highly sophisticated, ever-changing filtering system if it is to maintain its "purity" in the face of the world historic migration of women into it, and our education-gender system provides higher education with just this. The chilly classroom climate for women, the underrepresentation of women in the higher ranks of the professoriate, the backlash against women's studies, and the harassment of feminist scholars and scorn for their scholarship: these represent a small sampling of the mechanisms in operation in the academy. I single them out to show how harsh and brutal the system is. But they also command attention because they typify the trials by fire through which the feminist scholars I observed on my three philosophical expeditions had gone. Is it any wonder that survivors of these ordeals now make it their business to adapt to the academy's mores?

Chilly Classrooms for Women Students

Representing the plight of women undergraduates in his department, a Harvard University physics professor said in 1995:

> In the hard sciences, the undergraduate climate for women is a problem. In the case of physics, even though we've done a lot to improve them, those beginning courses for physics majors are a very macho environment. There are 120 kids, all of whom have always been the best students in their class in physics and math and chemistry, and they're a competitive lot. Trying to tone down that competitiveness a little bit is one of the most important things that we try to do for the climate.[1]

The coeducational classroom climate he described is not a uniquely Harvard occurrence nor is it limited to science classrooms. This device for filtering women, as the Atlantic crossing filtered nineteenth-century immigrants to the U.S., is a worldwide phenomenon that ranges over most, if not absolutely all, subject matters and levels of schooling and occurs in classrooms led by women as well as men.

In Sweden, ninth-grade boys boo when girls give wrong answers in science classes, sigh when the girls ask questions, and talk loudly when the girls give lengthy answers or introduce new subjects.[2] In the United States, a teacher calls a high school girl "airhead" and "ditz."[3] Meanwhile, reports from the United States and Australia tell of the blatant, demeaning, and continual sexual harassment of girls and women.[4] Studies of coeducation in several countries also show that at every educational level males and females behave differently and are treated differently by others including their teachers.

The different treatment of males and females within coeducational settings produces a chilly climate for women that takes myriad forms, extends beyond classrooms to school halls, lunchrooms, gymnasiums, playgrounds and athletic fields, residential settings, and extracurricular sites, and ranges over school experiences both great and small. Here are a few components of higher education's chilly classroom climate:

> › male and female teachers alike make eye contact with their male students far more often than with their female students;

> - male and female teachers more frequently assume postures of attentiveness toward the males, and call the male students by name more often than the women students;
> - male and female teachers call on the males more than on the females;
> - male and female teachers ask the males more difficult questions;
> - male and female teachers wait longer for the males to answer questions;
> - male and female teachers urge the males to try harder;
> - male and female teachers work with the males much more than with the females to elaborate answers to questions.

In addition,

> - male and female teachers are apt to address the class as if only males were present, interrupt women students and allow them to be interrupted by others, respond more extensively to questions put by male students, use examples that reinforce negative stereotypes of women, and make comments and tell jokes implying that women are not as competent as men.[5]

Women who have tried to alert colleagues to the hazards of the chilly climate know how hard it is for those who teach in the academy to credit its existence. As for making students aware of the problem, I will never forget the day I entered my philosophy of education classroom at the University of Massachusetts, Boston, prepared to lead a dispassionate discussion of the chilly coeducational classroom climate only to watch the behaviors listed by the authors of the landmark research on the topic be enacted before my eyes.[6] Nor can I possibly forget the course on gender and education, which I team-taught the year I was a visiting professor at the University of New Hampshire. There, my co-teacher and I met so much resistance to the chilly climate literature from our students—all of them women and each one convinced that her own choice of a teaching career had nothing to do with gender—that at my colleague's suggestion we sent them out to do their own research. The results of this small experiment in learning were spectacular. Even the most recalcitrant undergraduates were so incensed by the firsthand reports of sexual harassment from other women students, and so shaken by their own observations of the unequal classroom treatment of females, that their doubts evaporated.

The chilly coeducational climate does not lower the self-esteem and shake the self-confidence of *every* woman student. The mechanisms of the education-gender system are not that efficient. Indeed, some of us actually thrive on this kind of adversity. When, however, I read that a young woman at Duke University circa 1993 was asked on the very first day of her physics course, "Don't you feel out of place?"; and when I see what the professor included on her class's physics test:

> Starting with the lungs and using Bernoulli's equation, describe in full physical detail the production of the sound "Ohhh" by our lone sophomore female physics major. An anatomical sketch would be helpful.[7]

I know the time has come to face the facts. Although a chilly classroom climate affects different women differently, it impedes the academic achievement of many, causes numbers of women to desert mathematics, engineering, and science for "softer," more hospitable areas, and contributes to the high rate of attrition more generally.

I used to imagine it a simple matter to change the behaviors that contribute to the unfriendly classroom atmosphere. Yet even when grade-school teachers in England who were acquainted with the research findings made it their business to give the girls equal time and attention, they failed miserably in their intention. Each one left her classroom feeling quite certain that she had treated the two sexes equally, but independent observers timing the process reported that the girls had participated in discussions just over one third of the time.[8] In my own experience, whenever I sought equal time for the women students in my own classes I failed. On the day I tried my hardest to cajole and persuade the women to speak up, I only managed to antagonize them. "We like to listen. We learn more that way," they told me in no uncertain terms.

Listening to others is definitely a good thing and so is the "attentive and thoughtful" silence that one feminist scholar has so eloquently defended.[9] From years of university teaching I also know that many of those silent women learn at least as much of a course's content as do the unquiet men. Yet speaking as one who was herself a quiet student, I only wish that someone had long ago told me—and that I in turn had told my students—that shy college applicants turn into deferential, apologetic college seniors who then become muted graduate students.[10]

With the exception of one woman who later became a superstar of the intelligentsia, I do not recall ever hearing a female philosophy student voluntarily speak out in class when I was in graduate school. I certainly never did so myself, and I now know that this was not a healthy state of affairs. Surely I am not the only female who was tongue-tied in class and to this day remains so in similar situations. Besides, the overly talkative men students could not have profited from the silence of the quiet women. True, we women generously signed over to them the in-class practice time in philosophical discourse that we should have been using to develop our own skills. But the men needed practice in listening to us and to one another quite as much as we did in speaking out, and many of them also needed to learn self-restraint. If memory serves me, those who interrupted lectures and dominated discussions frequently seemed far more interested in hearing the sound of their own voices than in furthering the discussion and far more intent on impressing the professor and each other than on gaining insight into the topic. In looking back, it seems to me that more than a few of my fellow graduate students saw themselves in a kind of wrestling match with the professor for control of the class.

"What we see," say the authors of a study of women scholars, "is that women, faced with professional situations that demand authority, demand rebuttal, still attempt to please, to be winning, to be placatory."[11] I do not know how many of the women who dropped out of graduate school in my day might have acted differently had they demanded and been given equal conversational space. My guess is that if we had been made to feel like equal participants in the classroom process, and if the men's self-indulgent behavior had at the same time been curtailed, many more of us would have stayed the course.

I cannot say, either, just how the men students would have behaved in the changed circumstances. When, as a professor, I sought equal class time for women I discovered, as did those British researchers before me, that to encourage the equal participation of women and girls is to court the disruptive behavior of boys and men. My university students did not become noisy and obstreperous when the women were called on, as did the English boys in a similar situation, but they made their unhappiness about my quest for women's classroom equality quite clear. The men students in my classes made their discomfort even clearer when in the 1980s I began bringing materials on women into my philosophy courses. But this is to get ahead of my story.

A Hostile Climate for Women Professors

From the beginning, coeducation has taken different forms. Although at Oberlin College men and women initially followed curricula that had been designed to suit the different destinies in store for the two sexes, the variety of coeducation that finally prevailed was the model of mixed classes in which women and men studied what had formerly been men's curriculum. I need hardly add that for a long time they did so almost entirely under the instruction of male teachers.

Even now that women constitute 50 percent or more of student bodies across the world, men account for the greater part of the professoriate. My latest statistics from Sweden show that only 9 percent of university professors are women,[12] and a mathematician at Zurich University has calculated that at its present pace, it will take 11,406 years before women make up half that institution's professorial staff.[13] Granted, a more optimistic prognosis has been given for Harvard University. It is said that there it will take only forty years to achieve parity.[14] The truth is, however, that whereas countries like the United States and Britain appear to have much better records than, for example, Switzerland, Sweden, Norway, Denmark, Finland, Germany, France, Italy, Spain, Belgium, and the Netherlands, in these seemingly more enlightened nations women are over represented in the lower grades.[15]

Progress is slow. A detailed analysis of a 1988 survey of major U.S. institutions revealed that women then constituted 17 percent of the total professoriate and but 8 percent of full professors.[16] As of 1995, this latter figure stood at 10 percent for Yale and Michigan universities, 11 percent for Harvard, 12 percent for Princeton and the University of Wisconsin in Madison, and 13 percent for Stanford, Brown, and Columbia.[17] At the highest ranks everywhere there are many, many more men than women and, across the board, there is still a salary differential that favors men. In addition, women cluster in nontenured positions as adjuncts, part-timers, and instructors or lecturers. They are also concentrated in two-year institutions, are more likely to be teachers than researchers, and tend to be heavily represented in low-status fields.[18]

The reason usually given for the relative absence of women

in tenured positions is the lack of qualified candidates. It is true that some fields filter out women so efficiently that few end up in the pool from which the professoriate is ultimately drawn. Still, across the board a double standard operates in men's favor even as a hostile environment saps women's confidence and impedes our progress.

When women faculty at Canada's University of Western Ontario informed interviewers that the institution gave more time off for research leaves to men than women, they exposed to the light of day a practice that places higher demands on women than on men. Expecting the females but not the males in their ranks to teach a full course load while producing a body of scholarship whose excellence would earn them tenure, the university gave new content to the old double standard. Rather than require women to demonstrate a higher degree of sexual "purity," it set for them a higher standard of intellectual "prowess." The members of a philosophy department at a U.S. university participated in this same shady practice when they demanded that the leading female candidate for a position in ethics demonstrate mastery of the history of philosophy but placed no such requirement on the man still in the running. And so did the Swedish Medical Research Council when, in awarding postdoctorate fellowships, it held women to a much higher standard of scientific competence than men.[19]

But although I condemn the use of a double standard, I shrink from recommending one uniform standard for all. True, a double standard sets different expectations for women and men in situations where equity requires that the two sexes be treated in the same way. Nevertheless, a fixed single standard that is insensitive to gender issues does not invariably serve the interests of justice. Plato is the one who held that sex—or gender, as we would now call it—is a difference that makes no difference. He was absolutely right that it makes no difference where the ability to govern and the right to education are concerned. But in some contexts a person's gender can make a critical difference. As physicians are discovering, gender can make a very real difference to medical treatment. And, as students of human development are finding out, in the U.S. and many other cultures the career trajectories of men and women tend to differ because women are more likely than men to take time out for childbearing and rearing.

A U.S. study of ageism and antifeminism reports a "mommy tracking" of older, married women graduate students.[20] As one interviewee puts it, "the women who bear children during their Ph.D. work are not seen as part of the graduate student 'elite.'"[21] One Swedish scientist in turn tells an interviewer that she has come to accept that, with a family and children, her research advances more slowly than men's.[22] And another says of her husband: "When he was in the last phase of his Ph.D. it was very important, and he was not to be disturbed, and I had to do everything. But when I was in the same situation I still had to do everything."[23]

To look askance at a female candidate's application for an academic position because her career path diverges from that of males is in its own way as unjust as the imposition of a double standard. And the inequities of "the misplaced single standard" do not end there. I have seen women's typical ways of speaking and modes of behaving held against them in interview situations. In the case I remember best, a woman's unassertive demeanor was automatically interpreted as philosophical incompetence and her hesitant speech patterns as intellectual confusion.

Women in the professoriate repeatedly say how vital it is that there be at least one of our kind on every academic search committee. There needs be one of us on every research funding committee, too, and whether one of us is really enough is an open question. When a Swedish scientist was the lone woman on a research council committee, she learned "never to put forward any suggestions herself, but always to go through a man."[24] The day she wanted to elect another woman to the council, the men's reaction was: "But we shall really not have any bloody women's rule here."[25]

The paucity of women at the higher ranks of the professoriate makes the extra work a heavy burden, yet the alternative to eternal vigilance is apt to be the blithe disregard of job and grant applications from women. Indeed, women's "foreign" habits and customs make the presence of academic women imperative at the search stage and *every other* decisive point in the hiring, tenuring, and funding processes lest mannerisms having no bearing whatsoever on a woman's worth as a scholar or teacher are held against her.

Reports from the U.S. and Canada leave little room for doubt that women do not stop encountering problems once they are accepted into the professoriate. In fact, the academy's climate can be as chilly for women faculty who are hard at work within its confines as it is for women students. "I don't think that there's a day goes by that some kind of comment isn't made about my being a woman," one Canadian member of the academy told an interviewer.[26] Her colleague confided that when some men were discussing the hiring of women, one said: "Why do we need another woman, we've already got one."[27] Another faculty woman in Canada reported "an unending barrage of sexual jokes, sexual commentary, and sexist humor."[28] According to several of her colleagues, the experience of exclusion was a common one. Said one particularly successful professor: "The tacit agreement to steer clear of me was . . . underwritten by an odd deference. Evidently success, even success that reflected well on the department, wasn't grounds for admission to the boys club."[29] And there is also shocking evidence that the classroom itself can be a chilly environment for women faculty.

In view of our immigrant status, it is perhaps to be expected that some male students will express displeasure at being taught by women professors.[30] Given that our country of origin is the private home, it is not so surprising to find others addressing us as "dear."[31] But there is the case of an African-American female professor whose student—an off-duty police officer—carved her name on a bullet that he then proceeded to show to his classmates.[32] And as if this were not a sufficient sign of the academy's hostility to women, one study found 48 percent of female faculty reporting experiences of at least one form of sexual harassment by a student—the forms ranging from sexist comments to sexual assaults.[33]

One Canadian woman has summed up the chilly climate for women faculty created by students as follows:

> It's brutal for female faculty. They have to be enormously credible before students will listen to them. Male faculty might be viewed as eccentric, they might be ridiculed or imitated, but they would never be attacked as incompetent. For women, the connotation of incompetence is always tacked on.[34]

Indeed, it appears that the only group in the academy to be harassed more frequently than women faculty are women students.[35]

I consider myself lucky to have spent twenty years in the relatively friendly climate of the University of Massachusetts, Boston—friendly, that is, if one discounts:

the male student who mentioned menopause every time he spoke up in my class;

the male student who chose to interpret the questions I asked in order to promote my students' philosophical thinking as signs of my own ignorance of the subject;

the male colleague who wanted me to forego my own research project in order to work on his;

> the male colleague who for no apparent reason lashed out at me
> in utter fury at a department meeting;

and the myriad other episodes that in retrospect sound innocuous but at the time caused me great psychological distress. Having suffered these slings in a temperate zone and having visited more hostile ones—I have it on good authority that when I was a job applicant at a university in the Boston area a man on the search committee protested, "We've got too many broads already"—I am not surprised to learn that very few victims of harassment report the incidents.[36] Why on earth would one when the usual bureaucratic arrangements are unlikely to take seriously the daily assaults on self and psyche and when the more serious offenses are likely to be handled in ways that court reprisals? Knowing firsthand what it feels like to be ignored, slighted, publicly ridiculed, savagely denounced, and on top of all this treated as a sex object: I do not for a moment doubt that the careers of the victims of harassment are affected negatively or that these individuals are likely to experience sleep disturbances and nightmares, headaches, diarrhea, uncontrollable crying, agitation and restlessness, increased use of drugs, and deterioration in personal relationships.[37]

More research is needed to know if women faculty are apt to leave the most hostile campuses for friendlier ones—or for nonacademic environments—just as female undergraduate and graduate students migrate from the coldest classrooms into warmer climes. Indeed, more research is needed to know if the temperature is everywhere chillier for women in the professoriate than for men. After all, the fact that the climate of some institutions is intemperate does not mean that the whole of higher education is a chilly place for faculty women. We also need to ask in what ways the climate is different for women of color and for white women, for lesbians and for heterosexual women. And the question also remains of why the climate for women in the professoriate varies from school to school and from department to department. What makes it rise or fall? Are those classrooms chilliest for women faculty where the surrounding collegial environment is coldest? Does the presence of a significant number of women faculty in the environs affect the atmosphere and, if so, in what respects?

Despite all the unanswered questions, one thing is clear. The relative absence of women in the professoriate does make a difference to female students. Whatever doubts I may once have had on this score were laid to rest when, in fall 1995, I attended a philosophy department colloquium at the University of Oslo. Walking into a seminar room filled with more than thirty men and only two women, both of them graduate students, I felt myself transported back to my graduate-school days. The difference was that in 1960 I could not understand what I was experiencing. In 1995 I was able to name the overwhelming sense of oppression and the feelings of intimidation that came over me. In their wake, I could but marvel that a female would try to make a place for herself in a territory that had no senior women in residence, although I myself had done just that.

Calling the dearth of senior women in the mathematics department "an outrage," a participant in a 1995 round table discussion of women on the Harvard faculty said:

> People come here to concentrate in mathematics, and it's practically a violation of Harvard's contract not to say, "Please look at the names on your department catalog when you come in and understand that your likelihood of dropping out, of moving into sociology—the default option—is so high that we can tell you what the next four years are going to be like."[38]

After remarking that physics, mathematics, and engineering drive women out at an early stage of preparation, the lone man at the table reported that the relatively few women undergraduates in his department, physics, constantly speak of "feeling enormous pressure; being lone representatives of their gender in a hostile environment."[39]

In offering the opinion that "simply having some kind of critical mass of women in my department makes a huge difference,"[40] a Ph.D. student in comparative literature highlighted the fact that the absence of women faculty negatively affects students. The experience of having more than one role model gave her a sense of the possibility "that there are many different paths that a woman can take intellectually."[41] From the critical mass she must also have discovered that women have different ways of dealing with the recurrent theme of the women's group meetings run by the university, namely "the potential conflict between a professional academic life and a personal life."[42] Earlier in the discussion a woman professor in the history of science put her finger on one aspect of the difference that a critical mass of women in a department can make:

> It's gradually dawned on me during the past six or seven years that I've been at Harvard that I, without particularly setting out to do it, have apparently been modeling various things for the women graduate students in our department. One of the things I've been modeling is vulnerability and the need to find ways of coping with and overcoming vulnerability that comes from being a woman in a tough kind of a world, set up with rules that are not always friendly and comfortable to women and for women.[43]

I am walking proof that a woman can survive in the academy—indeed, live to tell the tale—without same-sex mentors and role models. Yet all these years I have been painfully aware of how many women philosophy students in my graduate-school days simply disappeared in the course of their studies or else left the field immediately thereafter. I sometimes speculate about how different our experience might have been had there been faculty members who even vaguely resembled us. Yet I cannot say for sure that the attrition rate would have been significantly reduced, for the education-gender system is remarkably adept at replacing one mechanism that filters out women by another.

Nevertheless, women students stand to benefit directly from

the presence of females in the professoriate, and they can also expect indirect gains. "It is difficult to think of women as illogical creatures when your logic or math teacher is a woman," writes one male philosopher.[44] As "the connotation of incompetence" fades away and patterns of behavior appropriate to male students of female professors emerge, the classroom climate for women faculty ought to improve. There is no guarantee that women-led classrooms will be more hospitable to women students than those led by men. In the long run, however, the shattering of the male students' deeply ingrained stereotypes of women[45] cannot but make the lives of both women teachers and students that much easier.

What constitutes an adequate representation of women in the professoriate? Some would like the percentage to correspond to women's percentage in the total population. Pointing to the scarcity of women in fields like mathematics and physics, others would have us settle for the percentage of women students in the various academic disciplines or else for the percentage of women Ph.D.s in those fields. The trouble with these last two standards of equity is that they give absolution to fields whose harsh climates send women into more temperate zones. Rather than require them to create conditions in which women can flourish, they implicitly condone the very practices that serve to filter women out. Yet if one opts for gender parity, as I am inclined to do, it is well to remember the reply a concerned young man gave when an undergraduate woman asked a panel of experts how long it would take for the Harvard faculty to be 50 percent female. In 1996, my student's question appeared to stun both audience and speakers. Into the shocked silence this cochair of Harvard's undergraduate student council dropped his considered opinion—one at odds with the oft-reported forty-year projection—that, at the present rate of tenuring women, parity would never be achieved. The indisputable fact made scarcely a ripple.

The unwillingness—or perhaps inability—to entertain the

notion of the very kind of parity that is now taken for granted in the case of coeducation is one sign that the historical project of bringing women into the professoriate is still in its early stages. Another such indication is that coeducation's counterpart on the faculty level has no name of its own. At least the English language has no word to indicate the mixing of the sexes on educational faculties as "coeducation" designates their mixing in student bodies. The obvious candidate "co-teaching" refers to team teaching. The term "co-researchers" is, in turn, reserved for collaborators on research projects.

An affirmative-action label is sometimes applied to the phenomenon to which I refer, but it is quite misleading. Government-sponsored affirmtive-action programs in the United States undoubtedly helped women gain entry into the professoriate, but that policy initiative is only one contributor to the development of what, for want of a better expression, I will henceforth call a "co-professoriate." After all, women's second entrance into the academy—our first entrance was as students—began in the U.S. in the nineteenth century and continues even as affirmative-action programs are being scuttled. It is, moreover, a worldwide phenomenon.

Quite aside from its historical and geographical limitations, the affirmative-action label often carries negative connotations. Call the hiring of a woman professor a case of affirmative action and many people will take it for granted that the academy has lowered its standards to admit her.[46] The label also deflects attention from the gendered character of the entrance of women into higher education as scholars and teachers. Even as it reveals the similarities between the situation of women and minorities, it hides the very factor that links together women's four entrances into the academy: first as students, next as faculty members, then as part of the curriculum's content or subject matter, and finally as feminist scholars. Use the language of affirmative action and it takes an enormous leap of imagination to relate the underrepresentation of women in the professoriate to the new gender tracking. Use the term "co-professoriate" and the tracking, the chilly coeducational classroom climate, the dearth of females in the professoriate, and the lack of a genuine "cocurriculum" come into focus together and can be seen for what they are: interconnected aspects of our education-gender system.

The Backlash against Women's Studies

Adrienne Rich once pointed out that the early feminists "assumed that the intellectual structure as well as the contents of the education available to men was viable: that is, enduring, universal, a discipline civilizing to the mind and sensitizing to the spirit."[47] Woolf knew better, but only in the 1970s did most feminists change their minds. Discovering for themselves that both the content and the structure of the various subjects of the liberal curriculum were male biased and realizing that women students are bound to be at a disadvantage when their lives and experiences are either misrepresented or entirely missing from their course of study, they took action.

Talk about heady times for feminist scholars! The years when academic inquiry into women's lives, works, and experiences was blossoming and the new scholarship on women was first being introduced into the liberal curriculum were as intoxicating as can be.

The excitement coincided with the arrival of the 1970s. A widely heralded analysis of the "sexual politics" of those four literary lions D. H. Lawrence, Henry Miller, Norman Mailer, and Jean Genet, appeared in 1969.[48] A now recognized classic paper, "Psychology Constructs the Female," maintaining that psychologists have nothing to say about what women are really like because they do not know, was published in 1971.[49] In 1975 a historian maintained that the conceptual models of history hitherto developed were all based "on the silent assumptions of a patriarchal ordering of values."[50] In 1976, a political theorist demonstrated that the field of politics relegated women, children, and the family to "the ontological basement."[51] In 1979, a biologist argued that Darwin had projected the Victorian picture of active males and passive females onto nature.[52] That same year a literary scholar wrote: "Feminist criticism cannot go around forever in men's ill-fitting hand-me-downs."[53]

These are just a few examples of the research documenting that women's lives, occupations, and achievements had been utterly excluded from the subject matter of the various fields or else had been seriously misrepresented. As the exposé of the very areas of knowledge that proclaimed their own impartiality, objectivity, and universality was extended to ever more fields of inquiry, a body of new scholarship about women's lives, works, and experiences emerged to correct the gender gap in knowledge. Carol Gilligan's *In a Different Voice*, published in 1982, is perhaps the best-known instance of the feminist research that went beyond critique of existing theory, but there were numerous others. In 1978 a literary critic asked readers to set aside the standard categories for evaluating fiction and see the sentimental novels written by nineteenth-century women in a new light.[54] Pointing out that the periodization in American history is irrelevant to women's past because it is based on political events, in 1979 a historian suggested that historians shift categories like "the New Deal" and "the Jacksonian era" to, for instance, "the ideology of family planning and contraception."[55] Meanwhile, scholars began writing treatises on child birth, housework, women's fiction, women scientists in America, and women's ways of knowing, to name some of the dozens—more likely hundreds or even thousands—of heretofore missing topics.

The new research program did not redress the unequal representation of women in the ranks of historians, philosophers, physicists, and the like. The aim was no more or less than the equal representation of women in knowledge itself: in the theories and hypotheses, narratives and interpretations, norms and methodologies that constitute the end products of academic inquiry. In other words, the object was to gain *epistemological equality* for women.[56] And the expectation was that if researchers and scholars devoted equal time and attention to women and women-related phenomena as their objects of study, the result would be the transformation of knowledge.

Actually, these were doubly heady times, for women's third entrance into the academy had a twofold aspect. What soon came to be known as the women's studies movement sought *curricular* as well as *epistemological* equality for women, and these are not the same thing.

The fact that research on women has been done in a given area does not necessarily mean that it will find its way into that field's curriculum. The fact that a given curriculum—for instance, the history curriculum of a girls' school—focuses on women does not mean that the corresponding discipline of knowledge, in this instance history, has established the habit of taking women as its objects of inquiry. People tend to think of curriculum as a mirror turned on knowledge. If it were one, then epistemological equality would automatically produce curricular equality. But although knowledge and curriculum are intimately related, the mirror metaphor is misleading.[57] As feminist scholars have discovered, although some forms of knowledge readily make their way into higher education's curriculum, others do not. In my experience, theories, and narratives that ignore or misrepresent women still seem to have easy access whereas ones that correct the male biases are frequently denied entry.

Even as feminist academics were attempting to close the epistemological gender gap by bringing women into the disciplines of knowledge, they set about trying to close the curricular gap by bringing us into higher education's course of study. Hence the establishment of women's studies programs in colleges and universities across the U.S. Hence, too, the efforts to mainstream the new scholarship on women across the entire liberal curriculum.

From the beginning, some feminists in the academy worried that to turn the study of women into a separate subject of the curriculum, which is what women's studies programs do, was to "ghettoize" the new research. Maintaining that material on women should be included in every subject of the liberal curriculum—if possible, in every course—they argued for the integration or mainstreaming of the new scholarship into all the disciplines.

Given that advocates of both the separate-subject and the mainstreaming approaches judged an "add women to the curriculum and stir" policy to be unsatisfactory and sought instead the transformation of the entire liberal curriculum, integrationism would seem to have been the better strategy. Stressing the interdisciplinary nature of women's studies,[58] defenders of women's studies as a separate or autonomous subject quite rightly pointed out, however, that mainstreaming accepted the very framework that needed to be transformed. In addition, autonomy's advocates argued that a women's studies person would encounter less interference with her research than would feminist scholars who belonged to existing departments.[59]

Actually, although supporters of the two strategies for radical curricular change sometimes gave the impression that the quite different approaches were mutually exclusive, these were—and still are—compatible policies. In fact they complement each other nicely.

Like any separate subject or department in the arts and sciences—for instance, history, physics, philosophy, anthropology, art, music—women's studies represents an enclave within a larger curricular structure, a region inhabited by a relatively small segment of the student population. Mainstreaming is a way of spreading the news collected by the various research projects on women. Yet vital as it is to distribute the study of women across the liberal curriculum, the very fact that women's studies programs are virtual enclaves enables them to function as safe havens for female students in an often hostile academic world. One member of that roundtable discussion of women at Harvard wondered how to move "from establishing, in a sense, safe zones, where we can begin to develop our scholarship and nurture graduate students, to a process in which they are going out and changing the broader university culture."[60] Safe asylum and outreach are both needed, and not only because the development of feminist scholarship and the nurturing of graduate students is so important. The climate for undergraduate women desperately needs to be improved and the integration of the study of women into all subjects of the curriculum is a crucial step in that direction.

If truth be told—and it too often is not—the two approaches to redressing the gender gap in the liberal curriculum need each other. And women in the academy in turn need both of them. Epistemological and curricular transformation have proved to be such elusive goals that it is a self-defeating policy to dismiss the one or the other out of hand.

Putting the worst possible face on women's studies programs—one that I, who for many years taught the seminar on feminist theory offered by my university's highly regarded women's studies program, fail to recognize—two feminist members of the professoriate did just this in 1994. Saying that they were not repudiating the study of women yet proposing no "middle way" by which to close the gender gaps in knowledge and curriculum, these scholars made mainstreaming the default option.[61] One has only to examine university course catalogues, however, to see what a small proportion of arts and sciences offerings include the study of women's lives, works, and experiences and to realize how little progress toward curricular equality mainstreaming has made to date.

The study of women is by now such a staple of higher education that people both inside and outside the academy are apt to assume that the gender gaps in knowledge and the curriculum have been closed. Yet despite the proliferation of women's studies programs since the 1970s, and notwithstanding the generous funding of some mainstreaming projects, the hoped-for transformations have not been accomplished. Even the far less ambitious goal of simply alerting students to the possibility of a gender bias in both knowledge and curriculum remains to be achieved. When in the 1980s I began teaching the feminist theory course, I quickly discovered that my students, most of whom were seniors, had never been introduced to the feminist critiques of their own disciplines and knew next to nothing about attempts to bring the study of women into history, literature, psychology, sociology, economics, and the like. Quite simply, if gender equality in the curriculum is to be achieved, we need to employ whatever strategies we can devise, for the University of Massachusetts, Boston, experience was not the exception but the rule.

That the high hopes of the pioneers of the women's studies movement have not yet been realized should be no surprise. Compared with the time it took coeducation to establish itself in institutions of higher learning, the progress already made toward a genuine *cocurriculum* would seem to be a case of spontaneous generation. In fact it now boggles my mind that those who participated in the women's studies movement expected that in just two or three decades a curriculum that had been designed by men and for men would be transformed—but in our euphoria, more than a few of us did. Now that I have identified the education-gender system and am able to see how it works, I consider our optimism especially misplaced. For when the object of education is assumed to be the preparation of students to take their places in the world of work, politics and the professions—a world traditionally inhabited by men and culturally defined in opposition to the world of the private home—it makes little sense to include the study of women or of women's traditional work in the curriculum. Indeed, it is positively irrational to do so.

Does the absence of a genuine cocurriculum at the level of higher education really matter? An African-American law student describes how she felt upon discovering the legal scholarship on race and gender that neither her own law studies nor her previous education had included in their curricula: "I cannot fully capture the full extent of my reaction to this discovery; it was akin to how most people have described a religious experience, or how a person born blind, through some miraculous medical procedure, becomes capable of seeing the world for the first time in her life."[62] A white undergraduate senior in the U.S. majoring in women's studies tells an interviewer:

> I think that Women's Studies definitely gave articulate words and a form to my amorphous anger that really had nowhere to begin to describe all that had happened to me. Through my Women's Studies classes I began to find coherent words to express my feelings, and I also had theories to back me up . . . I think that's the really big impact that the Women's Studies program has had on me, is that I've learned to speak up and not shut up when things bother me.[63]

Another graduating senior says: "I've always questioned everything, but Women's Studies has opened up whole new areas to question myself about. Questions like: 'Well, how is this useful for activism? How is this going to change the world? How am I implicated in this system of oppression, and what can I do about it? Am I working hard enough to change the world?' "[64]

A future lawyer discovers her roots by reading feminist research and scholarship. In women's studies classes one undergraduate woman finds her voice, the very thing that is so often lost in the classrooms of the academy's mainstream. Another walks away with a new and powerful intellectual framework in place. Start counting the ways in which the study of women can benefit young women and one begins to understand what a highly efficient and effective filter of women higher education's out-of-gender-balance curriculum is. Marveling at how far women had come in the last hundred years Woolf said: "It would have needed a very stalwart young woman in 1828 to disregard all those snubs and chidings and promises of prizes."[65] As I write, it needs a very stalwart young woman to see herself an active participant in the Promised Land when, from Day One, the official and hidden curricula of her education have bombarded her with messages to the contrary.

A woman who does not see herself on the syllabi and in the subject matter of her courses will not necessarily leave school. Multitudes who never once encountered a healthy, happy, productive woman in her official curriculum are living testimony to this. But from my own first acquaintance with the new research on women, from the emotional responses of so many of the undergraduate women I have taught, and from interviews conducted by students in a course I recently taught at Harvard on gender and higher education, I know how enormous the impact can be on one who finally sees herself and her concerns represented in the literature of her field. I know what a joy it is and how energizing it can be. I consider the magnitude of the jolt to be a measure of the damage done by the void in the standard course of study.

Like the gender gap in the professoriate, the gap in the curriculum deprives women students of positive mentors and role models. It reinforces in the minds of both sexes the prevailing view that women are not capable of doing meaningful work outside their private homes, let alone of doing significant scholarly research. And above all, by depriving women of contact with the very people and situations, the very topics and problems that they most readily identify with, it denies them emotionally charged studies. One can only speculate as to how many women might have been inspired to undertake academic pursuits of their own had they been able to see themselves in their course materials. From the standpoint of the education-gender system, of course, it is far better that women be denied the opportunity.

The Harassment of Feminist Scholars

Who knows! Had women in the 1970s been aware of the gendered underpinnings of the academy, let alone known how powerful and persistent our education-gender system is, the women's studies movement might never have been launched. Had anyone realized how well schooled in ignoring feminist deconstructions and reconstructions of their fields established scholars would prove to be and how easily theories and narratives whose androcentrism was demonstrated could be replaced by newer models of the same genre, the new scholarship on women might not have flourished. Had we feminist scholars entertained realistic estimates of the magnitude of the resistance to our efforts, we might have lost our nerve.

How many of us would have published our deconstructions and reconstructions of canonical knowledge had we expected this work to earn us hate mail, threatening telephone calls, and torched automobiles?[66] Would the feminist journals *Signs* and *Gender & Society* have ever been launched if their founders had foreseen their defacement and destruction in university libraries?[67] Would women's studies programs have even been developed if feminist scholars and teachers had anticipated the heckling, the defacing of posters and office doors, and the public displays of defamatory material that now occur?[68] I will not try to guess what might have happened—or rather, what might *not* have happened—had we had advance knowledge of the emergence of what in 1991 the Modern Language Association's Committee on the Status of Women called "antifeminist intellectual harassment."[69]

In a best-selling book published in the 1990s, Susan Faludi wrote that the antifeminist backlash in the U.S. of the 1980s had adopted many disguises, prime among them "a mask of mild derision."[70] Hate mail and car torching are simply the most dramatic masks that antifeminist intellectual harassment in the U.S. of the 1980s and 1990s has worn. Far less sensational but quite possibly every bit as effective is the derision that a handful of men *and* women have directed at both the epistemological and the curricular aspects of the study of women.

My Woman as Immigrant interpretation comes in handy here, for just as some nineteenth-century immigrants to the U.S. turned on their compatriots with scorn, a few women in the professoriate have engaged in antifeminist intellectual harassment. When I speculate about their reasons for joining in a pastime that seems to embody a form of self-hatred, I marvel at how closely the new arrivals in the Promised Land resemble those immigrants who, having "arrived" in America's mainstream culture, criticized and rebuffed their less assimilated compatriots. It was very hard to be a foreigner in New York or Boston or Chicago. It is equally difficult to be a woman in the professoriate today. Indeed, it is so hard that one can forgive those women scholars who wish away the scholarship and the courses that serve as reminders of their own presence in the academy.

The wish can be forgiven, but the harassment of feminist scholars and our work cannot be—not even when it dons the guise of mild derision. Woolf wanted the women who joined the procession across the bridge to act on the policy "that ridicule, obscurity and censure are preferable, for psychological reasons, to fame and praise."[71] How right she was that fame and praise can be dangerous things. What she did not say is that ridicule and censure can in their turn constitute intimidation.

"The hail of disdain poured on NOW's third-party proposal achieved its aim: extinguishing the spark of an idea before it had a change to spread," Faludi wrote,[72] and she added that the backlash "kept this historic political opportunity for women in check—with a steady strafing of ostracism, hostility, and ridicule."[73] A young woman recently confided to me that at a public lecture given by one of the country's most vocal deriders of feminist scholarship she felt as if the speaker was talking directly to her. "In editing a collection of essays about women thinkers, I am doing exactly what he was ridiculing. I am trying to bring women into the canon, and I don't want all the women to be white and middle class," she told me. Admitting that until the night of the lecture she had never thought of her research as having political implications, she said that she had suddenly become uneasy. With the essays already commissioned and a publishing contract in hand she said she would not be stopped—she was not stopped for the book is now in print—yet her demeanor testified to how quickly the excitement and enthusiasm generated by the scholarly study of women can be transmuted into that stark emotion—fear.

One object of the censure and ridicule directed at academic feminists is to keep research on women from being done. Another is to keep it out of higher education's curriculum. Consider that curriculum is the cultural equivalent of DNA and the reason for the virulent attacks on the project of transforming the liberal curriculum—indeed, on the very idea of a cocurriculum—is easy to fathom. Just as DNA passes down the genetic code, curriculum passes along the cultural code from one generation to the next by enabling knowledge to survive. If the new scholarship is taught in our nation's institutions of higher learning, the knowledge that casts doubt on the objectivity and universality of the old, familiar theories and narratives will take root and flourish. If, on the other hand, the offending knowledge can be kept out of the curriculum, that research will have a short life.[74]

"I was sure that the class would be filled with four or five hundred raging, die-hard feminists who would men bash telling of all the evils men have created. I guess you could say I was a little nervous," wrote a student in a journal she kept for an introductory women's studies course.[75] "At first I was disbelieving of the readings and the lecture, because I thought people were overreacting and finding excuses to be angry," recorded another.[76] In a Promised Land where fearful images of feminists abound, it takes a strong-minded undergraduate indeed to enroll in a single women's studies course. I marvel at the daring of one willing to declare women's studies as her field of concentration. And, as I have recently been astonished to learn, she who does enroll—and most of the students who prove strong enough are women—must also withstand pulls from parents who plead with their offspring to study more marketable subjects and pressures of another kind from the young men in their lives.

"To the conservative mind, lesbianism is the quintessence and ultimate aim of feminism," wrote the author of an analysis of anti-lesbian intellectual harassment in the academy.[77] Actually the false equation of feminism and lesbianism is tacitly accepted by men and women across the entire political spectrum. In a Promised Land where homophobia is rampant, what better way to prevent women from learning about their bodies and themselves? What better way to keep us from bonding with our own kind than to threaten us with the label "dyke"? What better way to intimidate classmates who want to take women's studies courses? What better way to threaten colleagues who would teach them?

Faludi pointed out that another mask of the backlash is "the painted face of deep 'concern.'"[78] Some of the parents who tell their daughters to major in French or economics instead of women's studies wear this guise and so do the authors of a widely advertised critique of women's studies programs that employs measured tones even as it likens them to Nazism, Stalinism, Maoism, and the purges of McCarthyism.[79]

If women's studies does not "acknowledge and address its considerable problems," it will "shrink into an introverted and marginal sect," those writers warn.[80] I might take the ominous predictions more seriously if they had applied their strict standards to the nonfeminist subjects of higher education's curriculum as well as to women's studies. In thrall to that same double standard that places higher expectations on women than on men, they entirely overlooked the introversion and marginality of so many academic departments and neglected to say that practically all the other separate subjects of the academy can also be portrayed in a dim light.

My object here is not to defend women's studies programs and courses from their critics, however. It is to remind both the friends and foes of feminism that the chilly climate for women's studies courses and feminist scholarship adversely affects women in the academy, whether they define themselves as feminists or not.

I also want to draw attention to the self-defeating habit of treating each of higher education's filtering devices on its own terms and in isolation from all the others. The reality is that these mechanisms of our education-gender system work in concert to maintain the "purity" of the Promised Land. The gender gap in the curriculum reinforces both the gender gap in the professoriate and the chilly classroom climate for women. The gender gap in the professoriate adversely affects the classroom climate and helps to maintain the gender gap in the curriculum. And the chilly classroom climate contributes to both the skewed composition of the professoriate and the continuing gender bias of the curriculum. Add more filtering devices to my list—for instance, the continuing attachment to what psychologists have called "separate" as opposed to "connected knowing";[81] the employment of pedagogies that make many women students uncomfortable;[82] the existence of a student culture steeped in romance;[83] and the devaluation of supporting staff most of whom are women—and the interconnections multiply. The reality also is that when old screening mechanisms wear out, new ones evolve to take their places.

CHAPTER IV

ASSIMILATION OR TRANSFORMATION, THAT IS THE QUESTION

It takes a stalwart young woman, indeed, to make it through these filtering devices. When I think of the determination and the dedication to scholarship academic women must possess just to come out on the other side intact, I marvel at the courage of those among them who choose to make the field of feminist scholarship their own. In an academy where the effects of the shock of women's immigration to men's world of paid work, politics, and the professions are still being felt, at the end of the day every woman deserves congratulations for her successes. Under the crisis conditions in which academic women live, feminist scholars scarcely deserve blame for trying to protect their newly won gains by putting their mastery of the academy's mores on display.

Near the end of *The Uprooted* Handlin asked: "No longer Europeans, could the immigrants then say that they belonged in America?"[1] Having survived higher education's sophisticated filtering system, can we feminist scholars say that we now belong in that sector of the world of paid work, politics, and the professions known as the academy?

In 1960 I returned home from an interview for an academic post at a major midwestern university only to be asked by a sociologist if a man had also been interviewed for the job. "I am sorry to say this," he told me, "but if so, they will hire him. Read *The Academic Marketplace*." They did hire him and in sheer disbelief—in those days I had no idea that a woman academic might be at a disadvantage—I read: "Women scholars are not taken seriously and cannot look forward to a normal professional career."[2]

Things have changed. Feminist scholars now hold conferences, publish journals, write encyclopedia entries, teach summer seminars. Nevertheless, the backdrop for these signs of success includes not only the attrition rate of women in higher education today, the new gender tracking, the chilly classroom climate for women students, the inadequate representation of women in the professoriate and the chilly climate for women faculty, the gender gaps in knowledge and curriculum, and the harassment of feminist scholars and their teaching—but the estrangement from women I discovered on my three philosophical expeditions.

It does neither women, men, nor the culture itself any good to gloss over the high price of belonging. I realize that the education gap in the feminist text keeps many feminist scholars in the dark about higher education's filtering mechanisms. I wonder, however, if even those who know the research on the subject see its application to their own cases.

Recalling her studies at the University of Sydney, Jill Ker Conway wrote in her autobiography, *The Road from Coorain*, "I read *The Origin of the Family, Private Property and the State*, treating its subject as though it were about some distant and different race rather than my own sex."[3] Explaining that she had "unthinkingly taken on the identity of the male writer and intellect present in all that I was reading," she said that she simply did not "take in emotionally" that the subordination of women which Engels had discussed applied to her. In similar fashion, we feminist scholars can read about higher education's filtering function without seeing the relevance to ourselves. Without wondering if we really did come through the process unscathed. Without ever realizing that as members of the academy we are now active agents in that selfsame process.

It does women, men, and the culture itself no good, either, to treat the academy's admission fee as part of the very nature of things. Nowhere is it writ in stone that, in the twenty-first century, the academy should continue to define its mission in terms of the nineteenth century's now obsolete split between man's and woman's worlds. Nowhere does it say that an institution that once excluded or devalued women-associated objects of study and inquiry must continue to do so. Nowhere does it say that members of the academy should uncomplainingly pay an admission fee that requires not just feminist scholars but all the academy's members to turn their backs on women.

With refreshing clarity, anthropologist Ralph Beals once distinguished between assimilation, which he described as a one-way process, and acculturation, which he called a two-way process: when acculturation occurs both parties to the transaction change, whereas in a clear case of assimilation an individual or group replaces its original culture with a new one.[4] Since, however, many experts have gone on using these two words interchangeably, with some adding the term "amalgamation" to the confusion, some calling cultural pluralism a theory of assimilation, and others viewing cultural pluralism as an alternative to same, scholars have injected various formulae into the discussion. Their stark simplicity sheds so much light on our subject that I will follow suit.

In these two equations, then, the letter A stands for the dominant or host group in a society and the letter B for an immigrant or ethnic group:

$$(1) \ A + B = A$$

$$(2) \ A + B = C$$

In the immigrant situation represented by A + B = A, when a new group is added to the host group, nothing changes. This equation portrays the one-way process Beals called assimilation. Historically speaking, it represents the ideology that prevailed in the U.S. when the nineteenth-century immigrants arrived.[5] Did those Irish, Italians, Germans, Jews, Poles, Norwegians, and Hungarians want to be accepted into the mainstream culture? If so, they would have to forego their own culture and adopt Anglo-Saxon behaviors and values. In the immigrant situation Beals called "acculturation," when an immigrant group is added to the host group, something brand new is forged. The equation A + B = C represents this state of affairs.

Now where women's acceptance by the academy is concerned, A + B = A represents current thinking. The idea implicit in A + B = C—that when women become full members of the academy a new and improved academic culture might be forged—may have been put forward by feminist scholars in the heady 1970s, but now it is rarely if ever entertained. Rather than thinking that the academy's mores might be enriched by women's presence, it is generally taken for granted that our belonging in the academy entails our conformity to the existing mores of the host society.

The trouble with this practically universal unspoken assumption is that our hosts' mores are predicated on estrangement from women. Indeed, the siphoning off of educated people, both male and female, from the activities and processes, duties and responsibilities, practices and institutions our culture associates with women is what our education-gender system is all about. Is the collective estrangement from women of feminist scholars in the very nature of things? Given the character of our education-gender system, when "things" are represented by A + B = A it most certainly is. But we can reject the prevailing meaning of "belonging" and opt instead for the formula

A + B = C. And if we do, estrangement need not be included in our membership fee.

Yet how realistic is it to ask immigrants to change the norms of their Promised Land? And given how difficult it is for women to gain acceptance by the academy, should we not in any case allow feminist scholars to rest on their laurels?

Occasional harassment and the life of a living contradiction may seem a small price for a feminist scholar to pay in return for a professorship and office of her own. But to these costs must be added the fact that the discrepancy between the lived experience of the great majority of women now in the academy and the euphoria regarding the status of feminist scholarship is not between us and unknown others. We once were women students. We now are women professors. The scholarship that was supposed to bring us epistemological and curricular equality was authored by us or our foremothers. The discrepancy is, in other words, between the several parts or aspects of ourselves.

Into the reckoning must also go coeducation's new gender tracking, the estrangement of feminist scholars from women on the track heading toward traditional "female" occupations, and what two researchers have called "the student culture of romance." "Men's prestige and correlated attractiveness come from the attention they receive from women and from success at sports, in school politics, and in other arenas. Women's prestige and correlated attractiveness come *only* from the attention they receive from men," wrote the authors of a report on women students at two universities in the U.S. South.[6] Actually, the culture they describe goes a bit beyond romance. True, the researchers report women "scheduling their classes on Tuesdays and Thursdays so as to be able to spend long weekends with their boyfriends, keeping weekend nights free in case their boyfriends want to go out, and deciding not to look seriously for a job after graduating because their boyfriends are not ready to leave the area."[7] However, some of the practices the young college women engage in eerily echo the early days of coeducation at Oberlin College. Then, it was official policy that women students make the men's beds. Today, no dean or provost tells women students to do the men's domestic labor. Yet as if in a race to be refeminized, college women "find time to wash their boyfriends' clothes, buy their food, clean their apartments, and work out refunds for repairs or defective purchases."[8]

In 1861, John Stuart Mill wrote: "Women who read, much more women who write, are, in the existing constitution of things, a contradiction and a disturbing element."[9] I think he would be pleased to know that women today are not only allowed to read and write with impunity, but are accepted by the academy as feminist scholars. But he would be dismayed to learn that, for all this progress, very different bodies of knowledge and skill and distinct traits of character are still built into our culture's stereotypes of masculinity and femininity.

"[You] may be able to do calculus, but I'm dating a football player," said one college woman to another.[10] What better way to dispel the embarrassment of having acquired some male-associated competencies than to drop out of the procession that heads up the hillside toward the occupations that used to belong exclusively to men and step instead into a new version of that old female role of wife and homemaker. What better way to escape the appearance of being a living contradiction.

Because social, economic, and political pressures quite outside the academy's control have more or less compelled it to accept some of us into its higher ranks, the academy's gender practices have shifted. Where once the outcome was the exclusion of women, it now is containment. What better mechanism for containing women could there possibly be than coeducation's new gender tracking. What better mechanism than the student culture of "romance."

Sadly enough, if we feminist scholars rest on our laurels, if having gone through trials of fire we say that other women should have to do the same, if having finally arrived in the academy we agree to keep our backs turned on our mothers, daughters, sisters, half-sisters, female cousins, and aunts: we aid and abet the academy's containment of other women and ourselves.

Add Women and Transform

CHAPTER 1

THE BRAIN
DRAIN

"If you can't stand the coldness of my sort of life, and the strain of it, go back to the gutter," Henry Higgins tells Eliza Dolittle in the very last scene of George Bernard Shaw's *Pygmalion*.[1] "Oh, it's a fine life, the life of the gutter. It's real: it's warm; it's violent; you can feel it through the thickest skin; you can taste it and smell it without any training or any work. Not like Science and Literature and Classical Music and Philosophy and Art." But Eliza has already said that she can't go back: "You told me, you know, that when a child is brought to a foreign country, it picks up the language in a few weeks, and forgets its own. Well, I am a child in your country. I have forgotten my own language, and can speak nothing but yours."[2]

In *Educating Rita*, Willy Russell's "rewrite" of *Pygmalion*, the heroine tells Frank, her university tutor, that her husband has burned all her books. "I see him lookin' at me sometimes, an' I know what he's thinkin', I do y'know, he's wonderin' where the girl he married has gone to. He even brings me presents sometimes, hopin' that the presents 'll make her come back. But she can't, because she's gone, an' I've taken her place."[3]

Who exactly has taken the earlier Rita's place? In Act One Frank explains to Rita why her very first effort at literary criticism is inadequate: "You must try to remember that criticism is purely objective. It should be approached almost as a science. It must be supported by reference to established literary critique. Criticism is never subjective and should not be confused with partisan interpretation. In criticism sentiment has no place."[4] At the end of the play's first act Rita asks if another effort of hers is rubbish. "No, no," Frank replies, "It's a totally honest, passionate account of your reaction to a play. It's an unashamedly emotional statement about a certain experience. . . . It's almost—erm—moving. But in terms of what you're asking me to teach you about passing exams . . . in those terms it's worthless."[5] By Act Two, things have changed. Upon reading Rita's latest essay Frank shrugs: "What I'm saying is that it's up to the minute, quite acceptable, trendy stuff about Blake; but there's nothing of you in there."[6]

Meanwhile a Mexican-American man, sitting in the reading room of the British Museum, is suddenly aware that there is nothing of him in the Ph.D. dissertation he is writing. Richard Rodriguez, whose depiction of the basic dilemma of higher education differs from Shaw's and Russell's accounts mainly in that theirs are fictional whereas his is not, reports in his educational autobiography, *Hunger of Memory*: "Whenever I started to write, I knew too much (and not enough) to be able to write anything but sentences that were overly cautious, timid, strained brittle under the heavy weight of footnotes and qualifications. I seemed unable to dare a passionate statement. I felt drawn by professionalism to the edge of sterility, capable of no more than pedantic, lifeless, unassailable prose."[7]

No, feminist scholars are not the only people who suffer estrangement at the academy's hands. Rodriguez tells of growing up in Sacramento, California in a Spanish-speaking family. Upon entering first grade he could understand perhaps fifty English words. Within the year his teachers convinced his parents to speak only English at home, and Rodriguez soon became fluent in the language. By the time he graduated from elementary school with citations galore, he had read hundreds of books. After graduating from high school he went on to attend Stanford University and, twenty years after his parents' decision to abandon their native tongue, there he was in the British Museum writing a dissertation in English literature. By any measure this is a success story, yet *Hunger of Memory* reads like a narrative of loss.

How else could it read given an education-gender system that turns men as well as women away from women? There is a wonderful account in *Hunger of Memory* of Rodriguez's grandmother telling him stories of her life. He is moved by the sounds she makes and by the message of intimacy her person transmits. He assures us, however, that her words themselves are not important to him. In fact, he perceives the private world in which she moves—the world of child-rearing and home-making—to be one of feeling and emotion, intimacy and connection, and hence a realm of the nonrational. In contrast, he sees the public world for which his education fit him as the realm of the rational. Feeling and emotion have no place in it and neither do intimacy and connection. Instead, analysis, critical thinking, and self-sufficiency are the dominant values. Needless to say, he ranks the one world and its associated attitudes and values far far above the other.

Rodriguez's education estranges him from women and women-associated phenomena, but it does much more than this. *Hunger of Memory* describes a journey of alienation: from Rodriguez's parents, for whom he soon has no names; from the Spanish language, in which he loses his childhood fluency; from his Mexican roots, in which he shows no interest; from his own feelings and emotions, which all but disappear as he learns to control them; from his body itself, as he discovers when he takes a construction job after his senior year in college.

My study of feminist scholars demonstrates how much light

the "abnormal"—in the sense of unusual—case can shed on the academy and so does Rodriguez's story. Of course, the academy's admission fee will vary according to each member's particular circumstances. A Mexican-American man will not pay exactly the same price as an African-American woman. A woman who devotes herself to mainstream research will not pay the same fee as one who does feminist scholarship. A man whose father is a professor will not pay the same price as one whose father is a manual laborer. In the U.S., one whose first language is English will not have to unlearn Spanish. Yet as I saw happen when I was teaching at the University of Massachusetts, Boston—it is a commuter school whose stated mission is to serve the community—the admission fee, which the academy exacts from all its members, bears a close resemblance to the one extorted from Rodriguez. Early in my career at UMassBoston, a philosophy major from one of the city's Irish-Catholic enclaves came to my office to say good-bye. Sitting in a neighborhood bar with his friends the night before, he had suddenly realized that if he continued his studies he would no longer be able to speak to them. In contrast to both Rodriguez and Rita, he was not willing to pay this price for a higher education.

John Dewey is the one who spent a lifetime trying to combat the tendency of Western philosophers and educators to divorce mind from body and reason from emotion. Rodriguez's educational autobiography documents these divorces and another one Dewey deplored—the separation of self from other. For even as *Hunger of Memory* depicts Rodriguez's journey away from his private home, it captures his progression from intimacy to isolation. Close ties with family members are dissolved with public anonymity replacing private attention. Rodriguez soon becomes a spectator in his own home as noise gives way to silence and connection to distance. School, says Rodriguez, bade him trust "lonely" reason primarily. And in school there is enough time and "silence," he adds, "to think about ideas (big ideas)."[8]

Admittedly, not every scholar has Rodriguez's good fortune to be born into a loving home filled with the warm sounds of intimacy, yet the separation and distance from parts of himself and from others that he ultimately experienced are not his alone. Dewey repeatedly pointed out that the distinction we in the U.S. draw between liberal and vocational education represents a separation of mind from body, of head from hand, of thought from action. Well, with few exceptions scholars are the recipients of a liberal, not a vocational, education—which means that just about all of us have been trained to be "disembodied minds." Granted, the concept of mind *can* be defined broadly enough to include feelings and emotions. However, the education our culture calls liberal aims at the development of rational mind and defines this narrowly. Thus are male and female scholars alike siphoned off from their bodies and themselves.

It is not surprising that Rodriguez acquired habits of quiet reflection rather than noisy activity, reasoned deliberation rather than spontaneous reaction, dispassionate inquiry rather then emotional response, abstract analytic theorizing rather than concrete storytelling. Culturally associated with men, these dispositions are integral to the scholarly ideal that has come down to us from Plato. In fact, upon completion of his educational journey Rodriguez bore a remarkable resemblance to the guardians of Plato's Just State. Through their education, those worthies acquire a wide range of theoretical knowledge, highly developed powers of reasoning, and the qualities of objectivity and emotional distance. Not one of Plato's guardians is the "disembodied mind" that Rodriguez became, for Plato believed that a strong mind requires a strong body. But Plato designed an education of heads, not hands, for his guardians even as he designed an education of hands, not heads, for his artisan class. Considering the passions to be unruly and untrustworthy, Plato also held up for the guardians an ideal of self-discipline and self-government in which reason keeps feeling and emotion under tight control. In other words, he emphasized "inner" harmony, not "outward" connection.

The great irony of the liberal education that comes down to us from Plato is that it is neither tolerant nor generous. As Rodriguez discovered, there is no place in it for education of the body, and since most action involves bodily movement, this means there is little room in it for education of action. Nor is there room for education of other-regarding feelings and emotions. The liberally educated person will be provided with knowledge about other people, but will not be taught to care about their welfare or to act kindly toward them. That person will be given some understanding of society but will not be taught to feel its injustices or even to be concerned over its fate. The liberally educated person will be an ivory tower person— one who can reason but has no desire to solve real problems in the real world—or else a technological person who likes to solve real problems but does not care about the solutions' consequences for real people and for the earth itself.

The case of Rodriguez illuminates several unhappy aspects of our Platonic heritage while concealing another. Those old enough to have seen Frederick Wiseman's 1968 documentary film, *High School,* may recall the woman who read to the assembled students a letter she had just received from a pupil in Vietnam. But for a few teachers who care, she tells her audience, Bob Walters, a sub-average student academically, "might have been a nobody." Instead, while awaiting a plane that is to drop him behind the Demilitarized Zone, he wrote her to say that he had made the school the beneficiary of his life insurance policy. "I am a little jittery right now," she read. She is not to worry about him, however, because "I am only a body doing a job." Measuring his worth as a human being by his provision for the school, she overlooked the fact that Bob Walters was taking pride in being an automaton.

The underside of a liberal education devoted to the development of disembodied minds is a vocational education whose business is the production of mindless bodies—a class division if there ever was one. In Plato's Just State where, because of their rational powers, the specially educated few will rule the many, a young man's image of himself as "only a body doing a job" is the desired one. But a democracy is not supposed to have two classes of people, those who think and those who do not. We are not supposed to have two kinds of people, those who rule and those who obey.

Actually, the academy's ideal inhabitants are heartless as well as disembodied, for in requiring the academy to turn its back on women, the education-gender system effectively banishes feelings and emotions from the scholarly realm. Or, to be more accurate, it rules these out except as they relate to intellectual inquiry. Yes, a scholar can care deeply about ideas and feel passionate about discovering the truth. After all, from a cultural standpoint these have long been considered men's concerns. The academy spurns just those feelings and emotions that have culturally and historically been attributed to women and the world of the private home.

The underside of an academy that tolerates the 3Cs of care, concern, and connection as they relate to ideas but not to other people, other living things, or the earth itself is a society whose trained intellectuals do not know how to respond directly to human needs, indeed do not even see the value of trying to do so. In a perfect world, this consequence of the academy's estrangement from women and women-associated phenomena might not matter. But we live in a world of child abuse and family violence, a world in which one of every four women will be raped at some time in her life, a world on the brink of nuclear and ecological disaster, a world of biological terrorism and ethnic cleansing, a world of poverty and economic scarcity. Too often, efforts to overcome these problems flounder under the direction of people who try hard to be rational, objective, autonomous agents but, like Plato's guardians, do not know how to sustain human relationships or respond directly to human needs, indeed, do not even see the value of trying to do so.

I recently had coffee with a college friend whose father had many years ago been both a Harvard professor and a key government official. Imagine my surprise when she turned to me and said: "Every time Dad returned from one of his trips to Washington, he would go to see his Harvard colleagues and, when he got home he would shake his head and tell us that they had no idea—not a shred of an idea—what the real world was like."

It would be a terrible mistake to suppose that members of the academy can single-handedly solve this world's problems. Still, just as a country becomes concerned when its scholars or engineers emigrate en masse to another land, I worry about the "brain drain" that occurs when members of the academy leave the real world behind. On my three philosophical expeditions the question on my mind was, What price women's belonging? I have since come to understand that this question is part of a larger one: What price does society pay for an academy that requires its members to turn their backs on women, men, children, and the world itself?

> > >

The aerial distance, the esoteric language, and the devaluation of the practical I saw on my second philosophical expedition are evidence of the academy's brain drain. On those travels I did not stop to think that the brain drain hurts everyone; that the whole society suffers when membership in the academy entails turning one's back on the problems of everyday life. I was so wrapped up in my study of women that I did not take note of the fact that men suffer too when the academy goes on the assumption that the best kind of theory is practice-independent; that the whole society suffers when the academy discards the vast amount of wisdom accumulated by women and men in everyday life.

Why do current discussions of higher education pay so little heed to the brain drain? One main reason is that the academy's dangerous practice of diverting the attention of society's "best and brightest" from the problems of the real world is closely bound up with our education-gender system. Culturally speaking, the aerial distance that makes it so difficult for members of the academy to see the problems of everyday life is considered to be a man's accomplishment not a woman's, and a very great accomplishment at that. Since, culturally speaking, the act of theorizing is also considered to be a man's work, not a woman's, the very idea that theory and practice are on a par challenges the prevailing cultural assumption that a male-associated activity is better than a female one. In addition, to try to unite reason with feeling and emotion is to challenge the cultural assignment of reason to men and feeling and emotion to women.

In other words, to stop the brain drain we must reject the gender labels our culture attaches to knowledge and skill, attitudes and values, personal traits and social practices. We must repudiate the prevailing cultural value hierarchy that ranks whatever is associated with men and boys higher than the things associated with women and girls. Given that whatever is culturally associated with females is also assigned by our culture to the world of the private home, we must also dispense with the education-gender system's two-world analysis.

In and of themselves, the benefits of stopping the brain drain warrant the dismantling of our education-gender system. Furthermore, the gains for women from ridding the academy of this obsolete apparatus can scarcely be exaggerated. Abandoning the beliefs and practices that render girls, women, and female-associated phenomena of all kinds anomalous within the academic scheme of things will help to make the coeducational classroom climate more temperate for women students and to create a more hospitable atmosphere for women faculty. It will reduce resistance to the integration of the study of women into the curriculum and increase the valuation now attaching to female-associated research entities. It will dilute the academy's hidden curriculum in misogyny and blunt the edges of its domephobia—its fear of and anxiety about things domestic. It will incorporate the 3Cs of care, concern, and connection to others into the academy's very definitions of what it means to become educated and perhaps even into what it means to be a good scholar.

Dismantling will do this and more. It will allow feminist scholars to gain acceptance in the academy without being siphoned off from other women, it will make full membership possible without our having to collude in the harsh and brutal filtering of other women, and it will end our period of servitude as tokens of gender equality rather than as concrete examples of the real thing. In other words, it will finally allow us to reach maturity.

Beals viewed the newly forged entity represented by C in our equation $A + B = C$ as a cultural blend, and this is what I have in mind when I call for a dismantling of our education-gender system. For $A + B = C$ to prevail, natives and newcomers alike will have to learn new ways. This does not mean that every woman in the academy will have to display *all* the dispositions of the natives or, conversely, that every man will have to acquire *all* the qualities culturally associated with the immigrants. For one thing, not all the traits and practices of either our hosts or ourselves deserve to be emulated. For another, some traits and practices may defy the blending process. All of which is to say that the new academic culture signified by C will necessarily be selective. This in turn means that the two parties to the transaction will be doubly affected: each will have to make a new array of characteristics its own, and, each will also have to shed old, familiar, but no longer desirable or functional traits and dispositions.

Now I can well imagine someone protesting that although equation A + B = C relates to the case of real-life immigrants, it does not bear on women's status in the academy. It is certainly true that women do not belong to a separate culture as did, for instance, those nineteenth-century Italians and Jews. It is true that we do not all participate in the same rites and rituals or partake of the same value systems and worldviews. I am well aware that to attribute one culture to all women is to fall into the trap of false generalization. I know full well that even to suggest that women's presence might enrich the culture of the academy is to activate the fear of refeminization and court accusations of essentialism.

However, to maintain, as I do here, that our culture still associates any number of attitudes and values, traits and dispositions, duties and obligations, skills and practices to women is not to generalize falsely or to be essentialist. It is to face the facts. My point is that our education-gender system now casts the many, many things culturally associated with women outside the academy's domain and at the same time deems so many of the things that fall within the academy's realm unwomanly. Only when that system is dismantled will the full range of praiseworthy human capacities become accessible to the academy and as available to the one gender as to the other.

Martha Nussbaum, a philosopher whose work I very much admire, has attempted to do what I say is impossible. In *Cultivating Humanity*, she has formulated an idea of liberal education whose goal, the cultivation of humanity, derives from Socrates's concept of the examined life, Aristotle's notion of reflective citizenship, and the classic Greek and Roman ideal of the world citizen. In defense of a reformed liberal education she first discusses what she takes to be the three essential aspects of cultivating humanity: the capacity for Socratic self-examination, the ability for people to see themselves "as human beings bound to all other human beings by ties of recognition and concern,"[9] and the capacity for narrative imagination. In a welcome departure from much present-day commentary on higher education, she then defends the inclusion of the study of non-Western cultures, African-American studies, women's studies, and the study of human sexuality in the liberal curriculum.

Perhaps because of Nussbaum's unbridled optimism where women's assimilation into the academy is concerned, she considers her own version of the historical project of extending to women an education originally designed for men unproblematic. Nussbaum reports that when she arrived at Harvard as a graduate student in 1969 women were not allowed to eat in the faculty club's main dining room.[10] But she seems to believe that with the equal admission of women students, with the hiring of more women than before onto faculties, and with the advent of scholarship about and by women, our worries are over.

In fact, the narrative about liberal education that Nussbaum herself constructs belies her claim that the study of women now pervades the academy.[11] Although her data include interviews with women students and visits to the classes of women faculty, the large story she tells about higher education is informed by the thinking of men. Granted, in addition to Socrates, Plato, Diogenes, Aristotle, Seneca, Marcus Aurelius, Epictetus, Rousseau, Kant, Tom Paine, Emerson, Thoreau, Whitman, Hilary Putnam, Nelson Goodman, and W.V.O. Quine, Nussbaum cites John Stuart Mill, a true feminist by my reckoning. But Virginia Woolf's *Three Guineas* and Adrienne Rich's essays on women's education might have shed additional light on her subject and so might my own reconstruction of a historical conversation about women's education in *Reclaiming a Conversation*, a book that Nussbaum once reviewed.[12]

A courageous defender of women's studies against its most severe and sarcastic critics, Nussbaum ends up exaggerating its successes—something some of its harshest critics have also done. An outspoken witness of the chilly classroom climate for women students at Notre Dame and the antifeminist harassment of women faculty at Brigham Young University, she gives her readers the impression that these are anomalous phenomena associated with religious institutions of higher learning. One who has read the literature on the subject will know that these cases are not special. They are merely particularly harsh instances of nationwide, indeed worldwide, practices.

Whether Nussbaum's optimism concerning women's status in the academy kept her from asking what from the standpoint of her own project are key questions, I do not know. She is in good company in assuming that an education designed for men can easily be extended to women without creating enormous problems for us. Plato, Wollstonecraft, and generations of nineteenth- and twentieth-century feminists did likewise. The fact is, however, that her book represents a missed opportunity. A passionate advocate of the critical examination of oneself and one's traditions, she never asks if the development of all the capacities that constitute "cultivating humanity" is consonant with the academy's mission as culturally defined. She does not ask how the extension to women of the capacities of logical analysis and reasoning for oneself—ones the culture has traditionally assigned to men—can be effected without forcing women to live out their lives as walking contradictions. She does not ask how the extension to men of the capacity of feeling connected to others—one our culture has assigned to women—can be accomplished given the academy's low regard of female-associated values and virtues.

I sing Nussbaum's praises for wanting to enlarge the scope of the liberal curriculum and applaud the democratic impulse that would extend this form of education to all. She does, however, overstate her case when she calls the idea of liberal education "a higher education that is a cultivation of the whole human being for the functions of citizenship and life generally."[13]

Liberal education as we know it is a cultivation of that part of the whole human being we call "mind." It is therefore telling that Nussbaum wants the products of liberal education to be intelligent participants in *debates about* the world's pressing problems but says nothing about their learning to participate in activities that might actually solve the problems. It is worthy of remark that although she promotes the ability to see oneself as a human being "bound to all other human beings by ties of recognition and concern," she says nothing about how human beings are to create and sustain such connections.

Because liberal education as we know it constitutes preparation for the world of work, politics, and the professions and places education for the world of the private home beyond the pale, it is also significant that although Nussbaum initially speaks of cultivating human beings for the functions of citizenship *and life generally*, the claims of world citizenship then command her full attention. To her credit, the everyday problems she wants the graduates of a liberal education to debate intelligently include what she refers to as "issues that seem close to home."[14] Yet she does not seem to notice the traps of aerial distance, esoteric language, and practice-independent theory, which those who wish to take these issues seriously regularly encounter. I, for one, will never forget the time I decided to include euthanasia in my course on contemporary moral and social problems. The philosophical writings on the subject were so technical, so far removed from the realities, and so unfeeling that I began to wonder if the literature I was asking my class to read would make it virtually impossible for them to enter into public discussions of the topic.

I do not myself see how a liberal education conceived of as cultivation for *the whole human being* can be realized by an academy that remains in thrall to the education-gender system that now prevails. I do not see how an idea of liberal education as cultivation for *the functions of life generally* can be put into practice if that system is not dismantled. Nussbaum's discussion illustrates the problem. She ignores the cultivation of human beings for living in families—in contrast to debating their structure; for regulating sexuality—as well as talking about it; for improving children's lives in addition to pondering this topic. The trouble is that in a society in which almost every man and woman walks across Woolf's bridge but returns each evening to some sort of home and family, everyone suffers from a form of education that excludes from its purview preparation for the one set of institutions and experiences. Nussbaum is right that many of our most pressing problems today have to do with issues traditionally associated with home. Yet what good is it to teach young people to debate the structure of families and the future of children intelligently without also cultivating their abilities to participate wisely and well in these practices?

CHAPTER 11

TALES OF
CONTAINMENT

For adolescent girls dissociation is a risky business. *Hunger of Memory* suggests that it was risky for Rodriguez too, and so, of course, it is for feminist scholars. From the standpoint of the containment of academic women in general and of feminist scholars in particular, however, our self-estrangement is heaven sent.

At an international meeting I attended in 1996, one graduate student after another reported troubling encounters with male colleagues and professors. The stories were shocking. Even more so was the fact that these budding feminist scholars had no idea what was happening to them and were surprised to discover that others were also being silenced in class, derided in public, and discouraged from making contact with leading feminist scholars in their field "for their own good." For a moment I thought I was on a fourth philosophical expedition, this one as a time traveler to an era before the groundbreaking pamphlet on higher education's chilly climate for women was published. Then I recalled what a keynote speaker had told her audience that very morning. Looking out on perhaps eighty people, only five of whom were men, she had said that she did not know if there were any women in the room.

Simone de Beauvoir's *The Second Sex* begins with the question, "Are there women, really?"[1] The doubt arose for de Beauvoir because the sciences "no longer admit the existence of unchangeably fixed entities that determine given characteristics, such as those ascribed to woman. . . ."[2] Our speaker would surely have seconded de Beauvoir's rejection of a female essence or essential nature and so do I. The difference between us is that she leaped from this denial to the very conclusion that de Beauvoir refused to draw. de Beauvoir wrote that to decline to accept a notion such as the eternal feminine "is not to deny that women exist today." To this she added: "this denial does not represent a liberation for those concerned, but rather a flight from reality."[3]

If those feminist scholars who have queried the existence of women had merely meant to remind us of the stereotypical content that has historically and culturally been embedded in the concept of women, their skepticism about the category *women* would not represent a flight from reality. This is precisely the kind of commentary that can give us a better grip on the everyday world. But rather than warn us about stereotypical conceptions of women, the skeptics bade us reject the concept *women* itself. The problem is that when feminist scholars affirm that we are not women we end up not knowing what to think or how to act when the rest of the world treats us as such. Since scholars who consider women to be a spurious classification can hardly be expected to inform their students about the earlier work on gender roles and stereotypes, we fail to prepare our successors for the gendered world in which they will live. Indeed, because those who deny that they are women are unlikely to imagine that the negative experiences they have in both the academy and the world beyond may be highly correlated with their gender, we set the stage for their bewilderment.

It might seem to be to a feminist scholar's advantage to refuse to identify herself as a woman. Will she not be beyond the reach of a colleague's misogynous outbursts? Can she not then slip easily through the horns of the dilemma of being an educated woman? These presumed achievements are illusory so long as the world persists in viewing her as a woman.

Our collective dissociation does more damage than this, however, for in distancing us from two important sources of self-understanding, it unwittingly contributes to our own containment. One source of self-understanding it denies us is studies of the kind done by Gilligan and her colleagues. Insisting that inquiries into the development of girls and women are essentialist, we have turned our backs on the very knowledge that illuminates our own behavior. Assuming that the related research of Jean Baker Miller and her associates on women's mental health and of Belenky, Clinchy, Goldberger, and Tarule on women's ways of knowing has no value, either, we cut ourselves off from precious insights into our thinking and ourselves.

Obviously, feminist research on female development leaves many questions unanswered. But no scholarly investigation has to answer every relevant question. Nor need a research program be flawless in order to serve as a fount of useful knowledge. Provided we do not take psychological inquiries by and about females as gospel; so long as we remember that no empirical studies can give us certainty: I know of no reason why we should separate ourselves from the knowledge they yield. On the contrary, this research can shed so much light on our beliefs, actions, and ways of being in the world that there is every reason to try to integrate its findings into our psyches and our lives.

Another invaluable kind of knowledge that our collective dissociation puts beyond our reach is provided by studies of exceptional women. Deciding in the 1980s that the 1970s search for notable women writers, artists, scientists, and political figures was misguided, one of the very first scholarly pitfalls feminist scholars flagged was the "women worthies" trap.[4]

Arguing that a focus on exceptional women ignored the masses and was therefore elitist, feminist academics told one another to stop searching history for women who come up to standards originally set by men and to start challenging the criteria against which women's excellence is measured.

Feminist scholarship has profited enormously from questioning the standard criteria of excellence, as well as by drawing its objects of research from all walks of life and all degrees of success. Still, there is nothing elitist about studying successful women. To be sure, if feminist scholarship were to restrict its research objects to women at the top, it would be guilty of the same sin that once infected men's scholarship. But to avoid elitism it is not necessary to shun the successful.

The toll this trap takes on our collective self-understanding is staggering. Social and behavioral scientists have long insisted that the abnormal case sheds light on the normal. By definition, extraordinary women are abnormal. If nothing else then, reflection on the life stories of those few who have risen from the ranks can enhance our understanding of the plight of the majority.

Citing Harriet Tubman, Sojourner Truth, Ida B. Wells-Barnett, Mary McLeod Bethune, Mary Church Terrell, Rosa Parks, among others, in 1970 Pauli Murray wrote: "Throughout the history of Black America, its women have been in the forefront of the struggle for human rights."[5] If any women are exceptional, they are. If any women were successful in their endeavors, they were. If any women's stories need to be told, theirs did. After reading Victoria Chambers's autobiographical *Mama's Girl* (1996), I would add that the study of the lives of successful women can offer insight into what it takes for a girl or woman to rise up, as it were, from poverty and abuse. Moreover, as a scholar who has striven to reclaim and reinterpret the educational philosophies of Wollstonecraft, Catharine Beecher, Charlotte Perkins Gilman, and Maria Montessori, I can also testify that the writings and life work of exceptional women of the past can have breathtaking relevance to one's own time.

Above all, because exceptional women are what we feminist academics are, whether we care to admit it or not, for us to turn our backs on this category can only contribute to our own containment. To shun studies of the successful is to cut ourselves off from knowledge of those past experiments in living in the Promised Land that were conducted by people very like ourselves. To be ignorant of how the educated women of this and earlier times solved the dilemma of being living contradictions is to be condemned to reinvent our lives and our work from one moment to the next.

Without perhaps meaning to, journalist Elsa Walsh documented three cases in point in a book called *Divided Lives*.[6] Focusing on women's experience, Walsh drew compelling portraits of three extremely successful women in the U.S. today. One of the unifying threads in her separate accounts of a TV personality, a breast surgeon at a major medical school hospital, and an orchestra conductor married to the governor of West Virginia is the virulent gender discrimination, not to say harassment, that these three women at the top encountered in their work lives. An equally striking aspect of their experience—and here I probably go beyond what the author perceived in her data—is these women's unpreparedness. Like the female graduate students at that international conference, these high achievers were utterly surprised at how their male colleagues and superiors acted; they did not know what to think or how to conduct themselves in the face of the sexist behavior; and, worst of all, there was no tradition, no body of lore, no collective wisdom to which they could look for help.

Walsh's women had friends and spouses who gave what advice they could, but they were not experts on gender matters: their firsthand experience was limited and their knowledge of the experiments in living conducted by other exceptional women was slight. Of course, Walsh's three were able to seek legal advice, but that is no substitute for the kind of help I have in mind. As I read Walsh's book I kept hoping that her women would find out how Florence Nightingale, Alice Hamilton, Jane Addams, and others in the past handled the dilemma of being and not being a woman. I kept imagining how much better off all of us who seek to make our homes in what used to be considered all-male professions might be if only we could have access to knowledge about how our contemporaries meet the challenges that confront living contradictions.

By the time I put the book down I was envisioning an archive in which was stored information about exceptional women's ways of coping with the problems inherent in their contradictory status. Because exceptional women differ from one another in so many respects my imagined depository quickly became a place in which records of the full range of available options were collected. I have only to recall the two high-ranking female officers in my university when I first arrived there to know that what works for one woman may not for another. Appearing to keep her own counsel, the one was direct, to the point, no frills, all business. Turning small talk into a fine art and seeking advice right and left, the other governed by indirection. The styles of these two exceptional women could not have diverged more yet each in her own way was a magnificent administrator.

Walsh's women had no Archive of Women's Ways of Coping in the Promised Land to consult and neither do feminist scholars. Still, the loss of understanding ourselves and our circumstances is not the most serious harm done us by our estrangement from women.

Not long ago a feminist scholar from another country asked me why a younger researcher in her field never cited her studies even though this compatriot knew that the older woman's work bore directly on her own investigations: Does she think I am essentialist or does she just want all the credit? Telling her that I had heard too many stories back home in the U.S. about feminist scholars either totally neglecting the writings of female colleagues or else casting them in a dim light to consider the oversight accidental, I confessed that in my opinion many of us were now acting as if we were in a competition with other women. It has since occurred to me that her two alternatives are not mutually exclusive. To call a theory essentialist is one way to take its author out of the running. Another way is to proceed as if her work does not exist. Still another, of course, is to misrepresent and then discredit it.

In view of how little room there is at the top of the academy for women, perhaps one should not be surprised to learn that feminist academics vie with each other for the existing space. Yet herein lies an irony. In 1972, Letty Cottin Pogrebin wrote: "Men compete for rewards and achievements; we compete for men." [7] As feminist scholars celebrate their arrival in the academy, women in the professoriate are competing not for husbands but, as the men do, for rewards and for the status attached to them. The problem is that because these goods are scarce and men control their distribution, we once again find ourselves competing with women. This time around, however, we vie with each other not *for* men, but *through* men—or rather, through those men we perceive to be our route to the approval and status we desire.

"We women have long been engaged in the enervating game of going every other woman one better," wrote Pogrebin. [8] Knowing how few women ever attain professorships and offices of their own, feminist scholars go every other woman one better when we engage in the practice of wholesale condemnation or follow a policy of non-citation. In our eyes the less said about another woman, the better off we ourselves will be. We also reduce other women's status whenever we apply the double standard and criticize women's work more harshly than men's.

Pogrebin reported that as a girl she was told to be charming—the formula for which was to look pretty, be clever and witty, and above all *"learn about what interests him."*[9] Confessing that she mastered this last only too well, she said, "In a profound sense, I am the sum of the boys and men whose interests I made my own."[10] The Promised Land's curriculum turns women into the sum of the male scholars and artists, humanists and scientists whose interests they have been required to make their own. When feminist scholars dismiss one another's work but take seriously the theories of men who neglect gender and misrepresent women, they are well on the way to adopting the academic interests of the men who control their fates.

Of course, I do not recommend that we cite works by women regardless of their quality or bearing on our subject. And, of course, to cite works by feminist scholars is not necessarily to overcome our estrangement from women for negative citation represents one way of "going a feminist colleague one better." True, insofar as the sheer number of citations a scholar receives is made the measure of his or her reputation—and it often is—negative citation is probably preferable to none at all. Still, if feminist scholarship is to grow and prosper, we need to connect our own work to that of others in more constructive ways.

One especially damaging consequence of a competition among women academics is that it compels new scholars to reinvent the wheel. At the conference in Sweden, a young student told us that when she looked at her data, she became confused. Although she had been taught to avoid the concept of patriarchy, patriarchy is what she saw. Her complaint was that she did not know how to proceed in her research. My concern is that feminist scholars may be leaving a whole cohort of women students in a state of near paralysis by condemning earlier feminist theory and research without providing adequate alternative modes of analysis.

Believing both women and gender to be spurious constructs,

the new generation of feminist academics is wont to steer clear of them. Told that earlier feminist theories and analyses falsely generalize and are essentialist—not to mention classist and racist—they do not read them. Warned that categories like patriarchy and male dominance are universalistic, they avoid them like the plague. Yet insofar as those up-and-coming scholars at the conference in Sweden had escaped the trap of aerial distance and were really looking at the world—and the women there were looking—they reported context after context, environment upon environment, in which men still dominated women and gender-equity was as elusive a goal as ever. With no tradition of how to talk about what they were seeing having been passed down to them—with the exciting insights into women's condition that feminist scholarship once produced now all but forgotten—they were floundering. Or else they were constructing brand new analyses that were even less sophisticated than those early presumed offenders.

Our dissociation from the work of other women, our unwillingness to situate our own research in relation to previous feminist work except to discredit it, our refusal to treat the body of feminist theory and research as a valuable intellectual resource: all this means that new feminist research is likely to lack both sophistication and grounding in feminist thought. These are steep prices to pay just to go each other one better. Far more costly still, the policies born of our intramural competition are ultimately self-defeating. At the Calgary conference where I presented the findings of my first philosophical expedition, the novelist Aretha van Hirk gave a rousing speech in which she asked why feminists are so intent on shooting themselves in the foot. The disconnection of our research from the work of other feminists does more than maim us. A method of containment par excellence, it is a form of mass suicide. It is no exaggeration to say that feminist scholarship which is not cited and used to good effect by other feminist scholars will ultimately disappear. If we do not cite and build upon each other's work, who on earth will?

> › › ›

Calling the story of her father's first years in America "the history of thousands," Mary Antin wrote in her autobiography:

> Dozens of these men pass under your eyes every day, my American friend, too absorbed in their honest affairs to notice the looks of suspicion which you cast at them, the repugnance with which you shrink from their touch. You see them shuffle from door to door with a basket of spools and buttons, or bending over the sizzling irons in a basement tailor shop, or rummaging in your trash can, or moving a pushcart from curb to curb, at the command of the burly policemen. "The Jew peddler!" you say, and dismiss him from your premises and from your thoughts.[11]

Elaborating on Antin's account of the immigrant plight, a contemporary of hers gave a description that fits women immigrants to men's world of work, politics, and the professions to a tee: "These people were not mere arrivals from the same family, to be welcomed as understood and long-loved, but strangers to the neighborhood, with whom a long process of settling down had to take place. For they brought with them their national and racial characters, and each new national quota had to wear slowly away the contempt with which its mere alienness got itself greeted."[12]

Where the academy is concerned, we women are new to the neighborhood. We, too, bring with us alien characteristics. We, too, have been greeted with contempt. For us, too, wearing away the contempt has proved to be a very slow and painful process. For us, as for all groups who seek admission into a Promised Land, the crucial question is: What does acceptance entail? And for feminist scholars there is the further question of whether to pay the academy's membership fee of estrangement from women.

Identifying seven types of assimilation,[13] Gordon concluded that when a minority arrives on the scene, a substantial change in the minority's cultural patterns—he called this "cultural assimilation"—is likely to be the first type of assimilation to occur. He also established that cultural assimilation tends to occur independently of the other forms and that its presence is no guarantee that the other types of assimilation will be achieved. Although the second and third generations of the immigrant groups he studied spoke English and had taken on American behavior patterns, by 1964 they had not achieved "structural assimilation"—large-scale entrance into the cliques, clubs, and institutions of the host society.[14] Intermarriage on a large scale had not taken place, either. Nor had the host society's prejudiced attitudes toward these immigrant groups or its discriminatory behavior been eradicated.

Gordon's analysis applies to feminist scholars. There is no need for me to review the notes that I took on my three treks across the academic realm to know that we have adopted our hosts' cultural patterns to a substantial degree. Had we not embraced the norms and practices of the natives, we could not possibly have earned our doctorates or published our articles and books. I did not have to go on three arduous field trips to know that in our case, too, cultural assimilation into the academy's attitudes, values, and practices does not necessarily spell acceptance. Yes, I have met women students and scholars who say they have experienced no prejudice in the academy and suffered no discrimination. And although I am not myself acquainted with female members of the professoriate who from the beginning were warmly welcomed into the academy's inner sanctums as understood and long-loved family members, I do not doubt such exist. But the chilly climate experienced by so many women students and faculty testifies to the host society's hostile attitudes and its unfriendly behavior. And the great resistance to the inclusion of women in both knowledge and curriculum, the dearth of women in the higher ranks of the professoriate, and our uneven distribution across academic departments all signify that large-scale structural assimilation has not yet occurred.

Because cultural assimilation is a matter of degree, it is natural for immigrant groups to assume that if they just try harder to acquire the natives' cultural patterns, they can speed up the entire assimilation process. In this spirit second-generation Americans shun their parents' mannerisms and reject their rites and rituals. It was for this reason that the nuns at Richard Rodriguez's local elementary school asked his parents to stop speaking Spanish at home. On my second philosophical expedition I marveled at the number of feminist scholars congregating near the traps of aerial distance, esoteric language, the devaluation of the practical, and the double standard. Gordon's analysis makes me wonder if we, as a group, are operating under the same misapprehension as those second-generation Americans. Are we feminist scholars under the impression that all we need to do to be accepted is to try harder? Do we too suffer under the illusion that a sufficiently high degree of cultural assimilation inevitably translates into structural assimilation?

Acknowledging that immigrant groups do not all follow the same pattern, Gordon explicitly excluded Northern and Western Europeans from his generalization. Maybe women are another exception to his rule. Perhaps we are the fortunate ones who, in the very act of making the academy's mores our own, actively promote the structural assimilation of our immigrant group.

The trouble with this happy conjecture is that cultural assimilation is the one type that requires few, if any, adjustments on the part of the host society. Keep adding to your repertoire of native behaviors and by your own efforts you increase your cultural assimilation. To achieve the other forms of assimilation the host must cooperate. So long as the natives persist in holding some characteristics of yours against you—in other words, so long as they remain prejudiced toward you—you will be unacceptable to them.

The question is: What, if anything, do our academic hosts hold against women? We women are in a double bind: whereas U.S. society held those nineteenth-century peasants in contempt for not being sufficiently like the natives, the academy is as apt to blame us for resembling them as for being different.

Remembering the progress made by women in the academy, some will think me unduly pessimistic about the prospects of structural assimilation. Considering my use of the term "containment" much too cynical, they will cite the well-known sociologist who has reported, "The incoming faculty member, in many fields, is now as likely to be female as male."[15] They will refer me to Nussbaum who wrote, "Scholarship about and by women pervades curricula, transforming not only the content but often also the methodology of established courses."[16] Can't you see how things have changed since your own undergraduate and graduate years, they will exclaim. Why call the glass of structural assimilation almost empty instead of nearly full when most history departments now boast a course on American women's history? When Romance language and literature departments offer courses in feminist literary criticism? When Austen, Eliot, Woolf, and Hurston have become standard fare in English departments across the nation?

I have only to open the 1996–97 course catalog of my alma mater's faculty of arts and sciences to know that things have changed. I have only to read the fine print, however, to discover evidence of institutional containment. I say "institutional" to flag the fact that I am not attributing a deliberate policy to the academy as a whole. Indeed, I do not even mean to suggest that the containment of women is an aim or goal of individual members of the academy. Rather, my point is that many practices of the academy produce outcomes that resemble those that would occur if the academy did subscribe to a deliberate policy of the containment of women.

On close reading of the catalog, I see that the enrollment of the Harvard English department's course Women and Religion in Late Medieval England is limited to fifteen, and that its courses on the Brontës, on Woolf, and on Sylvia Plath and Anne Sexton are similarly restricted. I also discover that the enrollment of the government department's single offering with the word "gender" in either its title or its course description is a junior-year seminar limited to sixteen students. And when I do a bit of elementary arithmetic I learn that the graduate seminar entitled "Seeing Difference: Feminist Theory and Modern Art" is taught by one of only two tenured women in a fine arts department that numbers twelve tenured men.

With mathematics on my mind I pull Blackwell's *A Companion to Philosophy of Religion* off my bookshelf.[17] Had this volume been published when I received my Ph.D. in 1961 there would have been no chapter on feminism, no index entry for this subject, and probably no women's names on the list of contributors. In 1997 I count eleven female authors and a whole chapter on feminism. This represents real progress, I say, and then the sobering facts hit home. This tome contains 78 chapters and the one on feminism is number 76. Chapter 76 is six pages long—less than 1 percent of the book's total length. The index to the volume contains no entry for "gender" and anyone with the temerity to look up "women" is referred to the entry on feminism. Of the four references to feminism in the index that are not to Chapter 76, three send the reader to fleeting mentions of the subject.

Wondering if this ponderous volume is atypical in its containment of women, I turn to an anthology in political philosophy also published in 1997.[18] At first glance, things look more promising. The index of what is advertised as a complement to the Blackwell *Companion to Philosophy Series* contains numerous references to feminism, gender, and women, and the majority of the seven selections authored by women appear to embrace a feminist perspective. Yet upon doing the relevant calculations, I realize that seven female-authored articles out of a total of thirty-eight is not so many—it is 18 1/2 percent to be precise. I also discover that, with one exception, the woman's paper comes last or next to last in its section; in other words, women again represent something of an afterthought. It seems that a little structural assimilation can create the illusion of being a great deal when one's starting point is the exclusionary policies of the past.

Gordon did not distinguish between the acceptance of individual members of an immigrant group into a host society's inner circles and the structural assimilation of that group as a whole, but it is helpful to do so. The tenuring of women scholars by highly regarded universities, the inclusion of works by women in major anthologies, the election of women to high office in professional societies: these do not in themselves signify the structural assimilation of women scholars more generally, let alone of feminist scholars and scholarship. After all, one good way for a host society to block the charge that it does not accept outsiders is to extend its welcome to a few select members of the alien group.

Like both containment and racism, tokenism can be the explicit policy of a social group or organization. Institutions can and often do respond quite cynically to charges of discrimination by performing symbolic acts designed to deflect the criticism rather than by seeking to effect significant change. They are frequently far too willing to hire a few individuals from the foreign group to whom they can then point with pride. But tokenism is often the unintended—although not necessarily the unwelcome—by-product of entrenched practice. Nobody in a university need say "Let's tenure one, or at most two, women per department; this should keep those strident feminists quiet" for the charge of tokenism to be valid. The gender—or for that matter the race or ethnic—distribution within the institution's tenured ranks will speak for itself. That is, it will do so provided one does a bit of arithmetic and also takes into account the contextual nature of structural assimilation.

Scanning a Boston Symphony Orchestra program booklet from the 1996–97 season in my new counting mode, I discovered that whereas women represented at least 50 percent of the first and second violin sections, there were no women at all in the brass and percussion sections or among the oboists, clarinetists, bassoonists, and double basses. While listening to Brahms I realized that the way the glass of assimilation appears to a beholder has a lot to do with one's reference point. The very situation that from the standpoint of a symphony orchestra's violin sections would be judged as full acceptance, represents tokenism when one adopts the perspective of the orchestra as a whole.

In regard to gender, Harvard in the 1996–97 season was remarkably like the Boston Symphony Orchestra: whereas women constituted 50 percent of the tenured faculty in the romance languages and literature department, women represented 11 percent of the tenured faculty of the government department, and anywhere from 4 percent to 8 percent in the mathematics department and the various science departments. Thus, from the standpoint of the romance languages and literature department, a significant degree of structural assimilation of women into the tenured ranks of the professoriate had presumably occurred. However, from the perspective of the faculty of arts and sciences as a whole, the equal gender distribution in romance languages and literature represented one more instance of tokenism.

Some will say that since Harvard is not your typical institution, I should disregard its dismal record regarding women. I disagree. Women in the academy, whether feminists or not, need to know that one of the world's most highly regarded institutions of higher learning practices gender tokenism. We also need to know that Harvard is not a law unto itself. Although its atypical tenuring system may aggravate its "woman problem," its treatment of women is not unique. Rather, it represents an especially egregious instance of a very broad pattern of discrimination and exclusion. I wager that if each and every one of us were to read her college or university catalog with gender on her mind and if we then pooled our knowledge, we would discover that gender tokenism is the rule in both the nation and the world.

Upon hearing me summarize my report to the Society of Feminist Scholars and Their Friends on the aerial distance and esoteric language traps, a researcher reminded me that feminist scholars have been keeping their distance from empirical data as well as from flesh-and-blood girls and women. To this, I would add that our deep disapproval of positivism has made us unduly suspicious of numbers. The quantitative study of gender bias in the application process for postdoctoral fellowships granted by the Swedish Medical Research Council ended with the recommendation that the secrecy of peer-review systems must be abandoned.[19] I learned an even more basic lesson from that stunning research, namely that women have much to gain from the relatively straightforward, seemingly unexciting work of recording numbers, calculating percentages, and running simple statistical tests.

I say "seemingly" unexciting because I, for one, found it thoroughly absorbing—albeit extremely depressing—to scan the Harvard catalog with an eye to determining the number and the distribution of courses about women and the percentage of tenured female professors. I wish I had the requisite training and skills, not to mention the material resources, to do the needed survey. Yet a "master" survey is not really required. If every feminist in the academy reviews her or his own school catalog, we will quickly find out both the good news and the bad. I think we already know the good news: things have changed. I very much fear that the bad news is that Harvard's problems are not its alone. Across the world there is a dearth of women in the professoriate and an underrepresentation of women in higher education's course content. This is a far, far greater disgrace, and we need to know the numbers.

CHAPTER III
ACTIONS
GREAT AND SMALL

At a conference on teaching I attended in 1998, a Chicano community organizer wanted to know about the book I was writing. When I told him that it had to do with feminist scholars losing sight of their dreams, he was visibly moved. "This is exactly what has been happening to Chicanos," he exclaimed. Some months before that meeting I had heard an African-American voice a similar concern about Afro-American studies departments. Quite clearly, the cause of women in the academy is the cause of minority men, too—and vice versa. Still, with gender equality at stake, women in the academy cannot afford to wait for men—be they minority or majority members—to act. To turn the academy into a woman-friendly institution, we must make the first moves—and who knows, perhaps the last ones as well.

What kind of transformation of the academy is needed for women to feel at home as students and professors? For us to achieve epistemological and curricular equality? For there to be a genuine co-professoriate? For feminist scholars to belong without turning their backs on their mothers, daughters, sisters, half-sisters, female cousins, and aunts? There is no one single correct idea of a transformed academy. On the contrary, an academy that dismantles the education-gender system so as to be equally hospitable to women and men and to admit both sexes into its inner sancta in equal numbers can take many different forms.

Given renewed interest in cultural pluralism, a solution to "the immigrant problem" that was so hotly debated in the early 1900s,[1] I should however make it clear that the equation $A + B = A + B$ does not represent the transformation of the academy I propose. This pluralist formula signifies a situation in which immigrant and host groups maintain their separate identities or cultures. Instead of being a blend of elements derived from host and immigrant groups, the resultant culture is no more or less than the sum of its parts.

In the case of women and the academy, however, $A + B = A + B$ perpetuates the estrangement from women and women-associated phenomena of both male and female scholars. Furthermore, the separation of men and women, which the formula signifies, replicates the stereotypical gender divisions that should be jettisoned. Research methodologies, conceptual frameworks, modes of teaching, patterns of curriculum all cut across actual gender lines. Yes, qualitative research methods are called "soft" and quantitative ones "hard," which in Western culture is tantamount to labeling the one feminine and the other masculine. But these attributions are artifacts of our education-gender system. Real men use both kinds of methods and so do real women. Speaking more generally, the stereotypical genderization of methods, theoretical schema, and the rest carries with it unwarranted denigration on the one hand and glorification on the other. But value judgments rooted mindlessly in gender are precisely what the academy should learn to do without.

One of the seven types of assimilation Gordon isolated was intermarriage. When I ask myself if this has any counterpart in the academy's case, I immediately think of the Shakespearean sonnet that begins, "Let me not to the marriage of true minds/Admit impediments . . ." The academic analog to marriage is the meeting of minds, the fruits of which are new ideas and theories. Intermarriage then represents a close communion of the minds of hosts and newcomers resulting in the birth of new ideas. By definition, the state of affairs signified by A + B = A + B does not countenance intermarriage between host and immigrant: each group authors its own theories and narratives and never the twain shall mix. Nor when A + B = A prevails is there intermarriage. Either our hosts ignore our work entirely or, like good daughters, we feminist scholars embrace the theories of famous men while hoping to adapt them to our own purposes. In neither case do we act like true adults. Nor is there true intermarriage. It would seem that only a transformed academy will admit no impediment to the intermarriage of true minds—at least when one of those minds is a woman's. And this, to me, is one more mark in its favor.

The ultimate shape that a transformed academy will take can no more be known in advance than can the details of the social and political strategies that ultimately produce it. Still, of this one thing I am certain. So long as feminist scholars are not just estranged from women in the outside world but divided from other women in the academy, the prospects of transformation will remain dim. One of our first moves must therefore be to reconnect with one another.

According to Gordon, those immigrant intellectuals, whose siphoning off so exercised him, did not become absorbed by the larger society; they were not for the most part admitted into its inner sancta. Rather, those writers, artists, and academics banded together into a "subsociety" of their own.[2] The experience of feminist scholars is quite different. The ghettoization/mainstreaming debate of the 1970s had to do with where in the academy the new scholarship on women should be located, not on the proper placement of feminist scholars themselves. To date, relatively little knowledge about women has been integrated into the curricula of arts and science departments, but we feminist scholars have ourselves been mainstreamed.

Given our expectation that we would be ghettoized in women's studies enclaves, our acceptance by the various arts and science departments can be judged a triumph. In light of the academy's institutional containment of women, however, the arrangement more or less insures that most feminist scholars will spend their days in splendid isolation from their own kind. In fact, it all but guarantees that women academics, whether feminist scholars or not, will be separated from one another. Our mainstreaming also means that, like wives in traditional families, most of us will identify and cast our lot with our separate, male-dominated units. Either that or be buffeted about by divided loyalties. Or rather, all this will happen if we do not join forces to prevent it.

Many academic professions now house feminist organizations which can serve to strengthen our identification with women and at the same time lessen our isolation. Indeed, the organization of this type that I know best, the Society for Women in Philosophy, is a veritable model of a feminist subsociety. Besides affording a forum for feminist philosophy by publishing a journal, sponsoring sessions at the yearly meetings of the American Philosophical Association, and holding local meetings every spring and fall, it provides participants with moral support, information about the profession, and a network of scholar friends. But even supposing that every academic discipline is equally blessed, the goal of reconnecting to women requires a broad range of subsocieties of our own, not just ones that are disciplinary based. We need groupings that cross disciplinary boundaries; that reconnect feminist scholars with women outside the academy's walls; that connect us with other academic women; that bring together academic women and women students; that create ties between and among women students, faculty, administrators, and staff.

On several visits to Sweden I have seen this last need met in part by an everyday occurrence called the *fika*. Every university department—indeed, every office and work unit—has its morning and afternoon *fika*, a time for coffee, cake, and conversation. There are those who do not attend, but most people appear to enjoy coming together with other members of their workplace to swap ideas, share troubles, and generally engage in talk both small and large about work, home, and world. Listening to feminist scholars in Sweden explain the *fika* in the abstract and realizing that I myself had been an occasional beneficiary of this institution, I began to think about what a feminist *fika* in my country might look like. Swedish coffee and cake would doubtless have to give way to their American counterparts and the frequency of the *fika* might also have to be adjusted. But these are minor matters. Intended as a way for feminist scholars to reconnect to women, the *fika* would bring the women of academe together to share gender-related troubles, plan courses of action, and swap ideas about women at work, at home, and in the world.

Are not the members of the academy in the U.S. too busy, too frazzled, and too overextended to spend valuable half hours with other women on a regular basis? The *fika* is so easy to establish and its potential benefits so great that some of us would surely be willing to try the experiment. My guess is that even where there are just one or two women in a department, departmentally based feminist *fikas* could make a major difference—and not just to the lives of the women who participate. My own experience of the good that ensued when a group of women faculty and students in the philosophy department at my own university broke bread together is what originally gave me high hopes. The action research that Mary Belenky, Lynne Bond, and Jacqueline Weinstock carried out in northern Vermont offers confirmation of my first impressions.

The Listening Partners project brought together isolated

mothers of small children living in rural poverty for weekly small group discussions where, over a period of eight months, they shared experiences, analyzed problems, and worked together to change their own lives.[3] The basic question Belenky and her colleagues wanted to explore was: "Would being a member of a group where people listen to each other with the greatest of care enable isolated mothers to gain a voice, claim the power of their good minds, and break out of their seclusion?"[4] The answer they give in *The Tradition That Has No Name* is an unqualified "Yes." As they report: "Having decided they had the capacity and the right to have a say in running their own lives, these women . . . began solving many of the problems that had been buffeting them and their families at every turn."[5] And in summation they say "By the time the Listening Partners project was completed we had accumulated a good deal of evidence that it is growth producing to have opportunities to speak in settings where people listen to each other and work collaboratively to solve the problems they face. This is particularly true for those who had been the most silenced and excluded."[6]

The women in Listening Partners stand so many worlds apart from feminist scholars that one wonders what we can possibly learn from their case. Examples of what the authors of *Women's Ways of Knowing* called "silenced women," these northern Vermonters "do not believe they are capable of learning from experiences mediated by language."[7] They also "think of themselves as 'voiceless' because they feel unable to give words to what they know."[8] Ironically, women in the academy today are in this same predicament: products of a highly verbal education, they are frequently unable to give words to what they know. Although the isolation of women scholars is not nearly so dire as that of these rural women in Vermont, we, too, may profit from hearing the stories of other women. We, too, may discover "how it makes you 'get beyond your own mess,' 'stop thinking just of yourself,' 'understand that you aren't the only one with these sorts of problems'."[9]

At the prototypes of the feminist *fika* in my own department, we twice created so supportive an atmosphere that students began to speak about the unspeakable: on both occasions a case of sexual harassment by an adjunct instructor was reported. Lest the cynics attribute this turn of events to the heat of the moment or to overactive female imaginations, I hasten to add that the accounts of harassment were later corroborated. I certainly hope that the incidence of sexual harassment in the academy is not so high as to make that experience the norm for feminist *fikas*. The question arises, however, of whether even an occasional revelation of sexual harassment at a feminist *fika* will place undue demands on women faculty. We already are overworked and underpaid. Does our reconnecting with the women in our respective departments mean that we must now serve as confidants and pillars of strength for students who have been victimized? Worse still, does it entail our having to run interference for our students with our colleagues?

The odds are great that the harassment of women, whether sexual or not, happens to our students—not to all, of course, but possibly to many more than most people think. The example feminist scholars set by shunning the unpleasantness—indeed, the example we set when we fail to create environments in which women are able to speak the facts—cannot possibly be in the best long-term interest of our students or ourselves. Fortunately, because the feminist *fika* brings together women faculty, students, staff, and administrators the burden of acting on the newly acquired knowledge will not be on feminist scholars alone.

Whatever subjects are discussed at feminist *fikas*, there will always be the possibility of these turning into occasions for women in the academy to wallow in their victimhood. The *fika* practice I envision does not deny that seeing oneself as a victim is a good antidote to the self-blame from which women still suffer. It does, however, adopt Bartky's analysis of the consciousness of victimization as a profoundly divided awareness: one sees oneself as victim but also has a consciousness of one's own power and the release of long-suppressed energy.[10] Should a student become aware of her victimization and make it known at a *fika*, in my scenario the other students in that small subsociety will decide—of course, only with her permission—to march together to the dean's office and report the case. Or they may decide to organize actions that circumvent officialdom.

> > >

Imagine this. A student says to the women in attendance at her department's feminist *fika*: "Listen to what happened in professor X's class today." Her *fika* friends quiet down and she proceeds: "All along, the classroom has had the atmosphere of a Donahue TV show. He calls on people and frightens them, but somehow students like it." There is a long pause. Then, fumbling with her can of diet soda, she whispers: "I like it." Another young woman now takes up the story: "I'm in the class, too. With him you don't get a word in edgewise. He's very imbalanced. Mad, then laughing. I'm scared. That's why I didn't say anything today." A third student chimes in. "Every time he sees me in the hall he says, 'When am I going to have you?' or 'You've been wanting me, I can see it in your eyes.'" At this point the first young women speaks up again: "You should see what he wrote on my essay: 'Short, but provocative.' Then today in class he read aloud a passage from a book on the syllabus. But first he said, 'I'm going to read this to you rough and slow . . . like they like it.' Turning to a guy in the class, he added, 'Don't they, Jim?' Next he read the passage: 'Black men kill for no reason and then ejaculate.'" "Last week," adds one of the other students, "he read us a long section on rape. I said, 'I can't believe we're actually being subjected to this,' and someone else started to say that the book is sexist. We tried to stop him, but he cut us both off."

There is no need to rehearse here the bureaucratic responses that the women faculty at this *fika* would encounter were they to usher a case like this through official channels. I do not say they should not try. But, back to our *fika*, suppose that faculty and staff members in attendance now tell the three students to stop making the usual excuses for their harassers, as they are beginning to do: to stop saying "He subjugates women, but . . . ," "He's degrading, but . . . ," "He just talks that way. You just have to learn to understand him. You have to overlook it." Suppose the women faculty and staff assure the students that they do not deserve to be treated in this way by their professors. Suppose one brave woman says that instead of sitting in class uncomplainingly the students should band together, make their plight public, and take joint action. And now, just suppose that someone has a copy of *Lysistrata* in her backpack. She pulls it out and reads aloud:

> The hope and salvation of Hellas lies with the WOMEN! . . .
> If we can meet and reach agreement
> here and now with the girls from Thebes and the Peloponnese,
> we'll form an alliance and save the States of Greece!
> . . . If I can devise a scheme for ending the war,
> I gather I have your support? . . .
> We can force our husbands to negotiate Peace,
> Ladies, by exercising steadfast Self-Control—
> By Total Abstinence . . .
> Here's how it works . . . Let's take the Oath to make this binding . . . Repeat after me:
> **I will withhold all rights of access or**
>   **entrance**
> **From every husband, lover, or casual acquaintance**
> **Who moves in my direction with erection.**[11]

In my scenario, the next time the instructor employs sexual innuendo to subjugate his students, a critical mass of women in his class rise as one person and exit en masse. From then until their grievance is redressed they refuse to attend class, do their assignments, or take their examinations. In other words, the women students bring Lysistrata into the classroom.

I have heard feminist scholars remind women who express concern about the academy's gender inequities of the need to be strategic. This, they say, is no time to rock the boat. Having reviewed my reports to the Society of Feminist Scholars and Their Friends and having begun to look at the numbers, I now reluctantly conclude that if women in the academy want equality, we will have to rock the boat.

To be a Lysistrata in the classroom is to rock the boat and act outrageously. And the classroom is not the only context in which women students can decide to be Lysistratas. Here is another scenario. At a reception for graduate students at which faculty members have been asked to talk about their own research, the sole women professor in the department is cut off by the chairman in the middle of her description of her projects for going over her time limit. Realizing that several male professors have already committed this same sin with impunity, the women students in attendance rise as one person to explain why the chair's action is unacceptable. When he ignores their protest, they walk out of the room—followed, I need hardly say, by the professor herself.

In quite a different scenario—one that Lysistrata did not herself adopt yet might well approve—student *fika* members publish an academic guidebook for distribution to incoming students. It supplies up-to-date facts and figures on the number and percentage of women faculty in the department and rates the department's classroom climates for women.

Give them time and humble departmental *fikas* might begin to generate small improvements in the academy's climate for both women students and faculty. They might generate larger ones, too. Belenky, Bond, and Weinstock tell us: "As people are drawn out and empowered they are likely to draw out and uplift others, who in turn will reach out to still others. If all goes well the chain might remain unbroken for many generations to come."[12] Still, in reconnecting to women it is not enough for feminist scholars to institute departmentally based subsocieties of our own. We need to cross disciplinary lines—something many of us used to do quite regularly. When I recently confided my worry about the confinement and isolation of feminist academics within their respective departments to some scholar friends, one ruefully recalled that, in the past, women faculty at her university met weekly for lunch. They no longer do, she told me. Another reminisced about the twice-yearly potluck supper meetings at which the women faculty at her university used to discuss a new feminist book. Surely, with a little bit of work, practices like these can be revived.

Here are two more scenarios, this time featuring women faculty. The first one begins over a potluck dinner with a female professor telling her colleagues about her department's most recent application of the double standard. It just so happens, she says, that besides having an excellent record and reputation, the highest-ranking female candidate for an advertised position in her department had published two books with one of the top university presses in the U.S. The highest-ranking man, on the other hand, had no publications to his credit. Nevertheless, after interviewing the two, her department decided in the man's favor.

Has anyone a similar event to report, she asks. It turns out that a surprising number do. There is, for instance, the case of a woman whose teaching contract is being terminated because students have been complaining about her foreign accent. A man in the same department with a much stronger accent is, however, being retained. There is also the case of a department's doubting the leading woman candidate's credentials for an advertised position but not the man's credentials, although the two attended the same graduate school, and she is the one with the more glowing recommendations. Agreeing that women faculty must follow the students' example and begin acting as Lysistratas themselves, those attending the potluck supper decide to file a protest at the next full faculty meeting. If, as they fear, their male colleagues ignore or belittle their efforts, they will walk out.

In my second scenario—it also takes place over a potluck meal—feminist scholars discuss the advisability of telling their women students something about their own lives and their ways of coping in academe. No one wants to make this compulsory for hesitant faculty. No one wants to force confidences on unwilling students. No one wants feminist scholars to indulge in true confessions or to wallow in a self-ascribed victimhood. The idea under discussion is simply whether it is a good idea for women scholars to present themselves to their students as people who live lives outside the academy—as people who have or do not have or may or may not even want to have lovers, husbands, children, parents, intimate friends.

I only began to understand how important this seemingly small yet for many academic women very scary step of self-representation might be when a Harvard undergraduate told me that she knew nothing about the private lives of her female professors—not even if they had children. Her teachers said nothing in class about themselves and were equally uninformative during office hours. I told her this goes with the territory: the academy does not consider the world of the private home its business. She replied that the silence troubled her because she was trying to decide whether or not to work for a doctorate and was wondering if it was possible to combine an academic career and children. At the very same time I was hearing this complaint, a student in my gender and higher education seminar was interviewing women faculty and discovering that, in their eyes, one of the main dilemmas they faced was how to combine life at home with a professorship of their own. She also found out that they were loath to speak to others about this problem.

In my scenario, the women faculty agree that students need a realistic picture of academic life so that they can make informed decisions about the future. One scholar says that they need to know that a woman can be a professor and the mother of young children, a professor in a heterosexual or a lesbian relationship, a professor who remains single throughout her life. Another insists they be made aware of the whole wide range of lifestyles available to academic women. A third thinks they need to know the difficulties that face any woman who walks across the bridge each morning to the academy and walks back home again at night. And all present agree that their students should be given a realistic reading of the chilly temperature for women in the halls of academe.

Feminist scholars have sometimes chided me for wanting to tell students about the way things are. You should not discourage them, they have said to me. The scholars in my scenario decide that to withhold the bad news from our women students is to act in bad faith. In fact, they also decide that to shrink from the phrase "It's the education-gender system" is to exhibit bad faith.

Years ago in a discussion of the methods of history, the philosopher William Dray isolated a form of explanation he called "colligation."[13] We tend to think of historical explanations as answers to "why" questions, but in actuality historians often explain *what* something is or *what* some series or group of events amounts to. They do so, Dray said, by bringing the phenomenon under some illuminating concept. In his memorable example, a historian when studying the events that took place in France in 1789 suddenly says, "Aha, it's a revolution!"

Feminist scholars have a choice. Maintaining that everything is itself and nothing else—a truism if there ever was one—we can continue to treat coeducation, the establishment of a genuine co-professoriate, the development of a thoroughgoing cocurriculum, and the integration of feminist scholarship as fundamentally disparate phenomena and leave it at that. And we can view the new gender tracking, the chilly classroom climate, the anti-intellectual feminist harassment and all the rest in the same way. Or we can colligate. We can pull together women's four entrances into the academy and the myriad problems associated with each one and say "It's an education-gender system!"

Colligation changes the picture. Call the academy's beliefs and practices an education-gender system and it is clear why all those past attempts to improve women's position were insufficient. For one can then see that an ideology of gender stereotypes and separate male and female worlds—or else separate sectors within the public world—informs just about every aspect of the academy we now know. Call it an education-gender system and one also gains insight into what must transpire if academic women are not to remain the tokens we all too often now are. It is not more and more cultural assimilation that is needed, with all the estrangement from women that this strategy entails. It is a transformation of the academy's underlying system of beliefs and practices.

The feminist scholars in my scenario urge their students to connect up with women from all walks of life in the academy and work with one another—and also with alumnae—to dismantle the system. They also place on their agenda the question of how to close the education gap in their text. Does each of us bring existing research on the education-gender system into every course we teach, or do we introduce a new course that is devoted to the subject? Should we send our students out into the academic community to do research on higher education as a filter of women or should we sponsor an academy-wide symposium on the subject? In the meantime, these scholars decide to create two archives: one will contain a file of women's ways of living their lives in the academy and dealing with the "divided lives" dilemma; the other will document women's experiences in the halls of academe and their myriad ways of coping well or badly with the chilly climate. Starting close to home, the scholars will offer up their own histories and will encourage their students to collect many more such for the files.

With our eyes on transformation, feminist scholars need to think across the disciplines and across college lines in order to make common cause with scholars on education, nursing, and social-work faculties. We also need to think both big and small, both strategic and outrageous. I realize that these terms are context dependent. From today's vantage point the opening of Harvard's Lamont Library to women seems a small enough event, but the deed took years to accomplish and, at the time, was considered by some to be utterly outrageous. In the future, the creation of archives may look like a small step but it will surely loom large in the eyes of its founders. Right now walking out of a classroom and into the dean's office is a huge step for one or a group of women students to take, but at some later date it might be so commonplace an occurrence as to be no more than a blip on the screen. Keeping in mind this caveat, I report here on what Heidi Weissmann did.

According to an interview in a 1996 issue of the *Women's Review of Books*, Weissmann's encounters with blatant gender discrimination when she was an associate professor of nuclear medicine at Albert Einstein College of Medicine easily matched those described in *Divided Lives*. Initially, Weissmann looked to professional circles for help. Sorely disappointed by their responses, she then turned to organizations like the Feminist Majority and the American Association of University Women. "It was very helpful to know that I wasn't alone," she said. "It provides tremendous sustenance to have moral support from organizations and individuals who believe in you."[14]

Awarded a sizable pretrial settlement but losing her medical school position in the bargain, Weissmann proceeded to establish the Center for Women in Medicine and Health Care whose purpose is to provide practical support for women faced with discrimination, harassment, and other forms of gender misconduct. Said Weissmann:

> I was not going to forget that there were other women out there who have to fight on these issues. I vowed that I was going to do what I could to share what I had learned. Women whose cases have come to a positive conclusion in part were able to do that because of resources they had within themselves, it's true, but also because of the network of other people that they were able to bring together to help them. But these are ad hoc networks centered on that case and that individual, and when it's over each of those people goes back to her or his own job and career, leaving the next woman to start all over from ground zero.[15]

Weissmann told her interviewer that at the turn of the twentieth century women could not get into medical school or make contributions but that now the problem has changed: "The problem now is to be able to protect these contributions."[16]

If it is necessary to think big just to protect the gains already made by women in the academy, how much more important it is if we are to make new progress. One outspoken student in my gender and higher education course asked a guest lecturer what she would do if her women's studies program were given $10 million. Our visitor had no answer. In fact, she appeared flabbergasted at the very idea of receiving so large a sum of money. Having just read in the mass media the rags to riches story of Harvard's department of Afro-American studies, I wondered why she did not take a leaf out of that book.

According to the *New York Times*, since the arrival at Harvard of literary scholar Henry Louis Gates Jr. in 1991, the department "has gone from a famously underachieving, largely unwanted stepchild at Harvard to perhaps the most celebrated assortment of scholars in America."[17] The *Times* article focused on Gates's brains and ambition, the high-profile colleagues he recruited, and the research and publication activities he directs at the W. E. B. Dubois Institute for Afro-American Research. In passing, it mentioned that Gates had so far raised $11 million for what banner headlines dubbed "Harvard's Black Studies Powerhouse."

Can a woman scholar raise as much money as Gates did? I can only say that to assume not without even trying is a counsel of despair. What might a feminist scholar do with a gift of $10 million? Following the Gates model, she could recruit an interdisciplinary group of distinguished scholars, all of whom agreed that "many great minds are better than a few."[18] Together with her high-profile colleagues, she could forge a community of scholars who believed in being "public intellectuals, people who are doing very, very careful work but are concerned about reaching a wide audience, people who are concerned about the direction of the country and are trying to influence public perception, public policy."[19]

If there were at her disposal no ready-made institute that awarded fellowships and sponsored major research projects, she and her team could establish one. There they could hold weekly meetings at which they could present working papers of their own, plan the next year's conferences, and map out new projects—all with a view to reconnecting feminist research to women in both the academy and the outside world. To implement their ideas they could sponsor workshops on the translation of the academy's esoteric languages into ordinary English—or Swedish, Spanish, Japanese as the case may be. And they could also invite feminist scholars such as bell hooks and Patricia Mann to discuss their research. Hooks and Mann are by no means the only members of the academy who have managed to avoid the trap of devaluing practice and the pitfall of a practice-independent theory. Our innovative gender institute might, however, want to launch a series of workshops on how scholars can stay in touch with the real world of women with an examination of these two women's ways of joining theory and practice.

In the introduction to *Micro-Politics: Agency in a Postfeminist Era* Mann explains that she formulated the theory of individual agency, which she unfolds in her book, in response to the changing gender relations that constitute "the most significant social phenomenon of our time."[20] She did not start out thinking that "we require new conceptual machinery."[21] Only after investigating the philosophical traditions of liberalism, Marxism, psychoanalysis, phenomenology and finding them "conceptually incapable of representing current issues associated with changing gender relationships"[22] did she begin to develop a theoretical framework that would "do justice to the social problems of our time." As she was rereading the relevant literatures, Mann could easily have lost sight of the real-life problems that motivated her theoretical endeavor. By keeping one eye on housework and familial relationships, pornography and abortion, date rape and sexual harassment, however, she managed to sustain an interactive conception of the theory/practice relationship. In consequence, she was able to propose new ways of thinking and acting in the real world.

Hooks has taken the lived experience of black women as both the point of departure for her own feminist theorizing and its point of return. "It was the dearth of material by and about black women that led me to begin the research and writing of *Ain't I a Woman: black women and feminism*. It is the absence of feminist theory that addresses margin and center that led me to write this book" she says in her preface to *Feminist Theory: from margin to center*.[23] The book at once reveals the limitations of existing feminist theories of parenting, education, work, power, violence, sisterhood and offers hooks's own account of each. Hooks could easily have lost sight of black women's realities as she moved far enough away to gain critical distance on them. In her preface she says, however, "Throughout the work my thoughts have been shaped by the conviction that feminism must become a mass-based political movement if it is to have a revolutionary, transformative impact on society."[24] And so she developed theoretical insights that can be turned back on the world to function as guides to feminist action.

At this institute feminist scholars could enter into conversation not just with other academics but with visitors from all walks of life. One of the very first visitors would be Heidi Weissmann. The names of high-profile scholars from home and abroad would, of course, be on the guest list. But low-profile scholars, and women in the arts, in politics, and in the professions—both those traditionally considered men's and the ones considered women's—would be included, too. And high on the list would be the names of community leaders and activists such as Jane Sapp, Rose Sanders, Jan Peterson, Patsy Turrini, Lorri Slepian, Monika Jaeckel, and Hildegard Schoos—the women whose work in building homelike public places is described in *A Tradition That Has No Name*.

CONCLUSION

To many people, the academy's implementation of the ideal of gender equality seems so simple a proposition, so moderate a desire as to require no deliberate plan of action—just an occasional reminder to women's well-meaning hosts. I thought so too until I saw a television documentary on the history of the suffrage movement in the U.S. that focused on how long it had taken women to attain the vote and how fierce the struggle had been. Some years earlier I had watched the same film with nary a thought about women and education. On this second viewing—it just happened to coincide with my teaching the gender and education seminar at Harvard—I began to see women's search for equality in the academy in a different light.

Watching that television documentary with women's higher education on my mind, I realized that attaining the vote for women was a world historic event and that women's entrance into the academy as the equals of men is of the same magnitude. If nothing else, then, the suffrage case teaches patience. I also learned from the comparison that although our struggle has already lasted much longer than we tend to admit, it will surely take even more time before it is done. Mainly, the comparison taught me to take comfort from the fact that although the struggle for the vote took well over a century, it did at long last succeed. Finally, and perhaps most important of all, the suffrage case made me understand that to effect a world historic change, it is necessary to call upon the whole range of political action.

I take heart from that often heartbreaking film on women's suffrage because, in the beginning, the very thought of giving women the vote made some men laugh and others cringe, yet the sons of those naysayers now take women's suffrage for granted. In the beginning, many women were made uneasy by the suffrage movement's "excesses," yet their daughters do not think twice about their right to vote. The suffrage movement gives me hope that, in the future, the very idea of an academy that welcomes feminist scholarship, a genuine co-professoriate, a true cocurriculum, and women-friendly classrooms will be taken for granted and the scorn and derision these now occasion will finally be laid to rest.

Or rather, the example of the women's suffrage movement gives me confidence that all this will happen *provided* women around the world decide that the academy's full acceptance of the ideal of gender equality is a cause worth fighting for. True, ours is a systemic problem of grand proportions. Practically everything about higher education is gendered. This is why the moment one problem is solved—the moment one inequality concerning women is eradicated—another crops up. At Oxford in the late-nineteenth and early-twentieth centuries, some dons and students derided the proposition that women be granted degrees and the university membership that this entailed while others reacted with unfeigned horror.[1] And, of course, many women insisted that the last thing they would ever want was an Oxford degree. Today the heirs of those men and women take women's right to earn degrees for granted. Now the scorn and derision are directed at feminist scholarship, at women in the professoriate, and at the move to integrate the study of women into both curriculum and knowledge.

Although the roots of our problem run deep, the suffrage example gives me hope. In Sweden I heard a feminist historian tell a group of researchers that she fluctuates wildly: one day she is an optimist about women in higher education and the next day she is a pessimist. I myself can fluctuate on the optimism question several times a day. When, however, I think of how outdated and dysfunctional is the academy's education-gender system and then recall the successes of the suffrage movement, my dismay at the academy's distance from the goal of parity is replaced by the firm conviction that we will at long last succeed. I do not imagine this happening in my lifetime or even the lifetimes of much younger women. But the suffrage case demonstrates that things do change when concerted action is brought to bear.

In the early days of the new scholarship on women, one of our number was moved to write an essay on the relationship between reform and revolution.[2] Today, feminist scholars rarely utter the word "reform" and revolution is the last thing on our minds. "Resistance" is the term of choice.

According to Foucault, whose reflections on resistance are often cited by scholars, "as soon as there's a relation of power there's a possibility of resistance."[3] Since he believed that power is everywhere, in Foucault's eyes so is the possibility of resistance. But although deeds of resistance can demand great courage and are not to be taken lightly, the fulfillment of women's dream of becoming equal, full-fledged members of the academy requires something more than this.

When I think about resistance as a political form, not a psychological process, I think of France during World War II. Members of the French Resistance were brave beyond belief. Of that I have no doubt. Nevertheless, theirs was a defensive operation developed in response to the Nazi occupation. "We're never trapped by power; it's always possible to modify its hold . . . ," wrote Foucault.[4] I hope he was right, but let us not forget women's high hopes for their scholarship. Let us acknowledge the high price now exacted from women for belonging in the academy. And let us finally admit that because of the academy's adherence to formula $A + B = A$ instead of $A + B = C$, gender equality has turned out to be a far more elusive goal than we anticipated.

To attain the vote for women, the suffrage movement ultimately employed the combined forces of self-described moderates who worked within the formal political system and of radicals both within and on the outside who, in the course of raising the public's consciousness about the existing system's injustices to women, made the moderates look like reasonable people. Acts of resistance played a part in the suffrage movement. However, the letters to newspapers, the marches, the caucuses, the mass meetings, the lecture tours, the shouting, the fastings, the forced feedings, added up to much, much more than resistance. They constituted a far-reaching and ultimately very aggressive campaign.

I do not know what the precise shape of a global campaign for a woman-friendly academy will be. No one can determine this in advance. What I do know is that the mass movement for suffrage included women who joined one march or attended a single meeting and women who devoted their careers and gave their lives to the cause. It was conducted by both women *and* men working both outside the formal political system and within. It consisted of acts both great and small, strategic and utterly outrageous. The cause of women in higher education— all women, of every race and group—demands no less, not one whit less.

NOTES

FOREWORD

1. Somer Brodribb, *Nothing Mat(t)ers: A Feminist Critique of Postmodernism* (Toronto: James Lorimer & Company, 1993).
2. Terry Lovell, Carol Wolkowitz, and Sonya Andermahr, eds. *A Glossary of Feminist Theory* (London: Arnold, 1997), 82.
3. Carol Gilligan, *In a Different Voice: Psychological Theory and Women's Development* (Boston, Mass.: Harvard University Press, 1982), 2.
4. Gloria Bird and Joy Harjo, eds., *Reinventing the Enemy's Language: North American Native Women's Writing* (New York: W. W. Norton & Co., 1997), 25.

ACKNOWLEDGMENTS

1. Jane Roland Martin, "Methodological Essentialism, False Difference, and Other Dangerous Traps," *Signs* 19 (1994), 630–57.
2. Jane Roland Martin, "Aerial Distance, Esotericism, and Other Closely Related Traps," *Signs* 21 (1996), 584–614.
3. Jane Roland Martin, "Bound for the Promised Land: The Gendered Character of Higher Education," *Duke Journal of Gender Law & Policy* 4 (1997), 3–26.

PREFACE

1. Margaret Mead, *Coming of Age in Samoa* (New York: William Morrow, 1928), 9.
2. Ibid., 11.
3. Ibid., 234.
4. Ibid., 13.

Notes

PART ONE: WHAT PRICE WOMEN'S BELONGING?

INTRODUCTION

1. Virginia Woolf, *A Room of One's Own* (New York: Harcourt Brace, 1929), 109.
2. Jane Gallop, Marianne Hirsch, and Nancy Miller, "Criticizing Feminist Criticism," in *Conflicts in Feminism,* eds. Marianne Hirsch and Evelyn Fox Keller (New York: Routledge, 1990), 355.
3. Ibid., 356.
4. Susan Bordo, "Feminism, Postmodernism, and Gender-Skepticism," in *Feminism/Postmodernism,* ed. Linda J. Nicholson (New York: Routledge, 1990), 148. Also Gloria Bowles, "Is Women's Studies an Academic Discipline?" in *Theories of Women's Studies,* eds. Gloria Bowles and Renate Duelli Klein (London: Routledge and Kegan Paul, 1983), 37.
5. Stephen Greenblatt and Giles Gunn, "Introduction," in *Redrawing the Boundaries,* ed. Stephen Greenblatt and Giles Gunn (New York: Modern Language Association of America, 1992), 1.
6. Jinhua Emma Teng, "The Construction of the 'Traditional Chine Woman' in the Western Academy: A Critical Review," *Signs* 22 (1996).
7. Virginia Woolf, *Three Guineas* (New York: Harcourt Brace Jovanovich, 1938), 60.
8. Ibid., 62.
9. Ibid., 72.
10. Ibid., 75.

I. ESTRANGEMENT FROM EACH OTHER

1. Robin Morgan, *Sisterhood Is Powerful* (New York: Vintage, 1970), xv.
2. Ibid., 637.
3. Shirley Chisholm, "Women Must Rebel," in *Voices of the New Feminism,* ed. Mary Lou Thompson (Boston: Beacon, 1970).
4. Michelle Zimbalist Rosaldo and Louise Lamphere, eds., *Woman, Culture & Society* (Stanford: Stanford University Press, 1974), vi.
5. Rayna R. Reiter, ed., *Toward an Anthropology of Women* (New York: Monthly Review Press, 1975), 11.
6. Nancy Chodorow, *The Reproduction of Mothering* (Berkeley: University of California Press, 1978), vii.
7. Julia Sherman and Evelyn Torton Beck, *The Prism of Sex* (Madison: University of Wisconsin Press, 1979), 8.
8. Susan Moller Okin, *Women in Western Political Thought* (Princeton: Princeton University Press, 1979), 5.
9. Peter Elbow, *Writing without Teachers* (New York: Oxford University Press, 1973), 177ff.
10. Linda Alcoff, "Cultural Feminism versus Post-Structuralism: The Identity Crisis in Feminist Theory," *Signs* 13 (1988): 411. See also Alice Echols, "The New Feminism of Yin and Yang," in *Powers of Desire,* eds. Ann Snitow, Christine Stansell, and Sharon Thompson (New York: Monthly Review Press, 1983), 439–59, and "The Taming of the Id: Feminist Sexual Politics, 1968–83," in *Pleasure and Danger,* ed. Carole S. Vance (Boston: Routledge & Kegan Paul, 1984), 50–72. Also Ann Snitow, "A Gender Diary," in *Conflicts in*

Feminism, eds. Marianne Hirsch and Evelyn Fox Keller (New York: Routledge, 1990), 17.

11. Jane Gallop, Marianne Hirsch, and Nancy Miller, "Criticizing Feminist Criticism," 353, and Teresa de Lauretis, "Upping the Anti [sic] in Feminist Theory," 255 in *Conflicts in Feminism,* eds. Marianne Hirsch and Evelyn Fox Keller (New York: Routledge, 1990).

12. Gayatri Chakravorty Spivak, "In a Word: Interview," *difference* 1 (1989), 128–29.

13. Jane Roland Martin, "Methodological Essentialism, False Difference, and Other Dangerous Traps," *Signs* 19 (1994), 630–57.

14. Jane Gallop, Marianne Hirsch, and Nancy Miller, "Criticizing Feminist Criticism," in *Conflicts in Feminism,* eds. Marianne Hirsch and Evelyn Fox Keller (New York: Routledge, 1990), 352.

15. Hester Eisenstein, *Contemporary Feminist Thought* (Boston: G.K. Hall, 1983), xviii.

16. See, for example, Elizabeth Spelman, *Inessential Woman* (Boston: Beacon Press, 1988), 158.

17. See, for example, Nancy Fraser and Linda J. Nicholson, "Social Criticism without Philosophy: An Encounter between Feminism and Postmodernism," in *Feminism/Postmodernism,* ed. Linda J. Nicholson (New York: Routledge, 1990), 30ff.

18. Ludwig Wittgenstein, *Philosophical Investigations* (New York: Macmillan, 1953), par. 66.

19. Ibid., par. 67.

20. bell hooks, *Ain't I a Woman* (Boston: South End Press, 1981), 137.

21. Ibid., 140.

22. Eisenstein, 133.

23. duCille, Ann, "The Occult of True Black Womanhood: Critical Demeanor and Black Feminist Studies," *Signs* 19 (1994), 591.

24. Susan Bordo, "Feminism, Postmodernism, and Gender-Skepticism," in *Feminism/Postmodernism,* ed. Linda J. Nicholson (New York: Routledge, 1990), 139.

25. Gloria Anzaldúa, ed., *Making Face, Making Soul* (San Francisco: aunt lute books, 1990).

26. Borob, 139.

27. Biddy Martin, "Feminism, Criticism, and Foucault," in *Feminism and Foucault,* eds. Irene Diamond and Lee Quinby (Boston: Northeastern University, 1988), xvii.

28. See, for example, Linda Kerber, "Some Cautionary Words for Historians," *Signs* 11 (1986): 301–10; Linda J. Nicholson, *Gender and History* (New York: Columbia University Press, 1986), 105; Joan Scott, *Gender and the Politics of History* (New York, Columbia University Press, 1988), 40; Nancy Fraser and Linda J. Nicholson, 32–33; Judith Stacey, "On Resistance, Ambivalence and Feminist Theory: A Response to Carol Gilligan," *Michigan Quarterly Review* XXIX (1990): 540.

29. Carol Gilligan, *In a Different Voice* (Cambridge: Harvard University Press, 1982).

30. See Carol Gilligan, Janie Victoria Ward, and Jill McLean Taylor, eds., *Mapping the Moral Domain* (Cambridge: Harvard University Press, 1988). Also Carol Gilligan, Nona P. Lyons, Trudy J. Hammer, *Making Connections* (Cambridge: Harvard University Press, 1990).

31. Elizabeth Gulbrandsen, "Objectivity? Reflexivity! Authority?!," in *Conditions of Our Knowing,* eds. Åsa Andersson and Hildur Kalman (Nordic Network for

Postgraduate Studies in Feminist Epistemology and Feminist Philosophy of Science: Umeå, Sweden, 1995), 79.

II. ESTRANGEMENT FROM WOMEN'S LIVED EXPERIENCE

1. Carol Cohn, "Sex and Death in the Rational World of Defense Intellectuals," *Signs* 12 (1987): 715.
2. Ibid., 716.
3. Ibid., 708.
4. Ibid., 704–705.
5. Ibid., 704.
6. Ibid.
7. Ibid., 705.
8. George Eliot, *Daniel Deronda* (London: Penguin Books, 1986/1876), 193.
9. Cohn, 708.
10. See Wendell Berry, *Standing by Words* (San Francisco: North Point Press, 1983), 37–38.
11. Cohn, 705.
12. Susan Schaller, *A Man without Words* (New York: Summit, 1991), 146.
13. Robert J. Lifton, "In a Dark Time," in *The Final Epidemic*, eds. Ruth Adams and Susan Cullen (Chicago: Educational Foundation for Nuclear Science, 1981), 9.
14. Ruth-Ellen Boetcher Joeres, "On Writing Feminist Academic Prose," *Signs* 17 (1992): 701.
15. Cohn, 713.
16. Michael Young, "Socially Organized Knowledge," in *Knowledge and Control*, ed. Michael F. D. Young (London: Collier Macmillan, 1971), 38.
17. Richard Rhodes, *The Making of the Atomic Bomb* (New York: Simon & Schuster, 1998), 761.
18. See Susan Bordo, "Feminism, Postmodernism, and Gender-Skepticism," in *Feminism/Postmodernism*, ed. Linda J. Nicholson (New York: Routledge, 1990), 133–56; Maria Lugones, "On the Logic of Pluralist Feminism," in *Feminist Ethics*, ed. Claudia Card (Lawrence, Kansas: University Press of Kansas, 1991), 35–44; Elizabeth Spelman, *Inessential Women* (Boston: Beacon Press, 1988); bell hooks, *Talking Back* (Boston: South End Press, 1989).
19. Holly A. Laird, "Editing Feminist Journals: Report on the October 1993 Conference, 'Publishing Feminist Scholarship,'" *Chain* 1 (Summer 1994): 74.
20. Ruth-Ellen Boetcher Joeres, 702.
21. Richard Jenkins, *Pierre Bourdieu* (London: Routledge, 1992), 169.
22. Ibid., 158–59.
23. Young, 38.
24. Thorstein Veblen, *The Higher Learning in America* (New Brunswick: Transaction Publishers, 1993), 21.
25. Scot Lehigh, "Universities Flunk Idea Test," *Boston Globe,* 3 March 1996: 69.
26. Kathryn Pyne Addelson, "Comment on Ringelheim's 'Women and the Holocaust': A Reconsideration of Research," *Signs* 12 (1987): 833. Also Kathryn Pyne Addelson, "Feminist Philosophy and the Women's Movement," *Hypatia* 9 (1994): 216–24.

27. See Maivân Clech Lâm, "Feeling Foreign in Feminism," *Signs* 19 (1994): 865–93.
28. Charlotte Bunch, "Not by Degrees: Feminist Theory and Education," *Quest* 5 (1979): 253.
29. Ibid., 251.
30. Virginia Woolf, "Mary Wollstonecraft," in *A Vindication of the Rights of Women*, ed. Carol H. Poston (New York: W. W. Norton, 1975) 221.
31. Barbara Carton, "A Rebel in the Sisterhood," *Boston Globe*, 16 June 1994: 69, 74.
32. Maria Lugones, "Playfulness, 'World'-Travelling, and Loving Perception," in *Making Face, Making Soul*, ed. Gloria Anzaldúa (San Francisco: aunt lute books, 1990), 392.
33. Sandra Harding, *The Science Question in Feminism* (Ithaca: Cornell University Press, 1986), 36.
34. Ibid., 39.

III. Estrangement from "Women's" Occupations

1. Jean-Jacques Rousseau, *Emile*, trans. Allan Bloom (New York: Basic Books, 1979), 40.
2. Susan Brownmiller, *Femininity* (New York: Ballantine, 1984), 17.
3. Dorothy C. Holland and Margaret A. Eisenhart, *Educated in Romance* (Chicago: University of Chicago Press, 1990), 132.
4. Naomi Wolf, *Fire with Fire* (New York: Ballantine, 1993), 213.
5. Audre Lorde, *Sister Outsider* (Trumansberg, New York: The Crossing Press, 1984), 61.
6. Sandra Bartky, *Femininity and Domination* (New York: Routledge, 1990), 15.
7. Ibid., 16.

Part Two: An Immigrant Interpretation

I. Women as Immigrants

1. Nancy Fraser and Linda J. Nicholson, "Social Criticism without Philosophy: An Encounter between Feminism and Postmodernism," in *Feminism/Postmodernism* (New York: Routledge, 1990), 32.
2. Carol Gilligan, Nona P. Lyons, and Trudy J. Hammer, eds., *Making Connections* (Cambridge: Harvard University Press, 1990), 10.
3. Carol Gilligan, "Joining the Resistance," *Michigan Quarterly Review* XXIX (1990): 501.
4. Ibid., 502.
5. Ibid., 530. See also Lyn Mike Brown and Carol Gilligan, *Meeting at the Crossroads* (Cambridge: Harvard University Press, 1992).
6. Carol Gilligan, "Hearing the Difference: Theorizing Connection," *Hypatia* 10 (1995): 124.
7. Carol Gilligan, "The Centrality of Relationship in Human Development: A Puzzle, Some Evidence, and a Theory," in *Development and Vulnerability in Close Relationships*, eds. Gil Noam and Kurt Fisher (New York: Lawrence Erlbaum, 1996), 247.
8. Gilligan, 1990, 522.

9. Ibid., 523.

10. Gilligan et al., 1990, 11.

11. Judith Stacey, "On Resistance, Ambivalence and Feminist Theory: A Response to Carol Gilligan," *Michigan Quarterly Review* XXIX (1990): 540.

12. Brown and Gilligan, 215.

13. Milton M. Gordon, *Assimilation in American Life* (New York: Oxford University Press, 1964), 256.

14. Ibid.

15. Oscar Handlin, *The Uprooted* (Boston: Little Brown, 1951), 4.

16. Ibid., 5.

17. Mary Antin, *The Promised Land* (New York: Penguin Books, 1997), 270.

18. Ibid., 271.

19. Ibid.

20. Handlin, 5.

21. Ibid., 5–6.

22. Ibid., 6.

23. Kim Thomas, *Gender and Subject in Higher Education* (Buckingham: Open University Press, 1990), 124.

24. Joann Muller, "Crimson-faced," *Boston Globe,* 22 April 1998: F5.

25. Kevin Cullen, "Breaking Thin Blue Line of Bias," *Boston Globe,* 16 January 1996: 20.

26. Lisa Disch and Mary Jo Kane, "When a Looker Is Really a Bitch: Lisa Olson, Sport and the Heterosexual Matrix," *Signs* 21 (1996): 278.

27. Reuters, "Women Testify on Lewd and Harassing Behavior on Wall Street," *Boston Globe,* 23 January 1998: C2.

28. Handlin, 6.

29. Ibid., 61.

30. Ibid., 39–40.

31. Ibid., 61.

II. THE NEW GENDER TRACKING

1. Inger Munkhammar, *What Does Public Statistics on Education Tell?* (Stockholm: Statistics Sweden, 1996). See also "Shared Power, Responsibility," (National Report by the Government of Sweden for the Fourth World Conference on Women in Beijing, 1995).

2. Suzanne Stiver Lie and Virginia O'Leary, eds., *Storming the Tower* (London: Kogan Page, 1990). See also Miriam K. Chamberlain, ed., *Women in Academe* (New York: Russell Sage Foundation, 1988).

3. "Women Account for Half of College Enrollment in U.S., Three Other Nations," *Chronicle of Higher Education,* 17 September 1986.

4. *Doctoral Recipients from United States Universities* (Washington D.C.: National Research Council, 1987).

5. Barbara Solomon, *In the Company of Educated Women* (New Haven: Yale University Press, 1985), 1.

6. Ibid.

7. Martha West, "History Lessons," *Women's Review of Books,* February 1996: 21.

8. Jane Roland Martin, *Changing the Educational Landscape* (New York: Routledge, 1994), Chap. #3, 5.

9. Evelyn Fox Keller, *A Feeling for the Organism* (San Francisco: W.H. Freeman, 1983), 141.

10. Anthony Tommasini, "Academy Strings Ensemble Even Better 'Live,'" *Boston Globe,* 8 October 1988: 16.

III. HIGHER EDUCATION AS FILTER

1. "Women on the Faculty," *Radcliffe Quarterly* (Fall/Winter 1995): 14.

2. Else-Marie Staberg, "Gender and Science in the Swedish Compulsory School," *Gender and Education* 6 (1994).

3. Myra Sadker and David Sadker, *Failing at Fairness* (New York: Touchstone, 1995), 134.

4. See, for example, Margaret Clark, *The Great Divide* (Canberra: Curriculum Development Centre, 1989); Peggy Orenstein, *SchoolGirls* (New York: Doubleday, 1994); Nan Stein and Lisa Sjpostrom, *Flirting or Hurting?* (Washington D.C.: National Education Association, 1994).

5. Roberta M. Hall and Bernice Resnick Sandler, *The Classroom Climate: A Chilly One for Women* (Washington D.C.: Association of Women's Colleges, 1982). See also Bernice Resnick Sandler, Lisa A. Silverberg, and Roberta M. Hall, *The Chilly Classroom Climate: A Guide to Improve the Education of Women* (Washington D.C.: National Association for Women in Education, 1996).

6. Hall and Sandler, 1982. See also Sandler et al., 1996.

7. Sandler et al., 33.

8. Dale Spender, *Invisible Women* (London: Writers and Readers Publishing, 1982), Chap. #4.

9. Patrocino P. Schweickart, "Speech Is Silver, Silence Is Gold," in *Knowledge, Difference, and Power,* eds. Nancy Goldberger, Jill Tarule, Blythe Clinchy, and Mary Belenky (New York: Basic Books, 1996), 305–31.

10. Nadya Aisenberg and Mona Harrington, *Women of Academe* (Amherst: University of Massachusetts Press, 1988), 68.

11. Ibid.

12. Inger Munkhammer, *What Does Public Statistics on Education Tell?* (Stockholm: Statistics Sweden, 1996).

13. Inga Bogstad and Elin Svenneby, eds., "Gender—an Issue for Philosophy?," (Oslo: Second Nordic Symposium of Women in Philosophy, 1994).

14. Kimberly McLarin, "Radcliffe Alumnae Get Tough with Harvard," *New York Times,* 7 January 1996: 39.

15. Suzanne Stiver Lie and Virginia O'Leary, eds., *Storming the Tower* (London: Kogan Page, 1990), 25.

16. Jennie Farley, "Women Professors in the USA: Where Are They?," in *Storming the Tower,* eds. Suzanne Stiver Lie and Virgiania O'Leary (London: Kogan Page, 1990), 198.

17 "Women on the Faculty," 17.

18. Annette Koldony, "Paying the Price of Antifeminist Intellectual Harassment," in *Anti-Feminism in the Academy,* eds. VèVè Clark, Hairley Nelson

Garner, Margaret Higonnet, and Ketu H. Katrak (New York: Routledge, 1996), 24.

19. C. Wennerås and A. Wold, "Nepotism and Sexism in Peer Review," *Nature* 387 (1997): 341–43.

20. Mary Wilson Carpenter, "Female Grotesques in Academia," in *Anti-Feminism in the Academy*, eds. VèVè Clark, Hairley Nelson Garner, Margaret Higonnet, and Ketu H. Katrak (New York: Routledge, 1996), 158.

21. Ibid., 149.

22. Sylvia Benckert and Else-Marie Staberg, "Is It Really Worthwhile? Women Chemists and Physicists in Sweden," in *Education into the 21st Century*, eds. Alison Mackinnon, Inga Elgqvist-Saltzman, and Alison Prentice (London: Falmer Press, 1998), 122.

23. Ibid., 125.

24. Ibid., 128.

25. Ibid.

26. Constance Backhouse, Roma Harris, Gillian Michell, and Alison Wylie, *The Chilly Climate for Faculty Women at UWO: Postscript to the Backhouse Report* (London, Ontario: University of Western Ontario, 1989), 26.

27. Ibid.

28. Ibid., 34.

29. Ibid., 30.

30. Ibid., 21.

31. Ibid.

32. Patricia Williams, "Talking about Race, Talking about Gender, Talking about How We Talk," in *Anti-Feminism in the Academy*, eds. VèVè Clark, Hairley Nelson Garner, Margaret Higonnet, and Ketu H. Katrak (New York: Routledge, 1996), 81.

33. Greta Gaard, "Anti-Lesbian Intellectual Harassment in the Academy," in *Anti-Feminism in the Academy*, eds. VèVè Clark, Hairley Nelson Garner, Margaret Higonnet, and Ketu H. Katrak (New York: Routledge, 1996), 117.

34. Backhouse et al., 21.

35. Gaard, 117.

36. Ibid., 118.

37. Ibid., 119.

38. "Women on the Faculty," 12.

39. Ibid., 14.

40. Ibid., 13.

41. Ibid.

42. Ibid., 16.

43. Ibid., 13–14.

44. Michael Martin, "Pedagogical Arguments for Preferential Hiring and Tenuring of Women Teachers in the University," in *Women and Philosophy*, eds. Carol Gould and Marx Wartofsky (New York: G.P. Putnams Sons, 1976), 329.

45. Ibid.

46. See Benckert and Staberg, 1998.

47. Adrienne Rich, "Toward a Woman-Centered University," in *On Lies, Secrets, and Silence* (New York: W. W. Norton, 1979), 131.

48. Kate Millet, *Sexual Politics* (New York: Ballantine, 1969).

49. Naomi Weisstein, "Psychology Constructs the Female," in *Woman in Sexist Society*, eds., Vivian Gornick and Barbara K. Moran (New York: Basic Books, 1971), 133–46.

50. Gerda Lerner, "Placing Woman in History," in *Liberating Women's History*, ed. Berenice A. Carroll (Urbana: University of Illinois Press, 1976), 364.

51. Lorenne Clark, "The Rights of Women: The Theory and Practice of the Ideology of Male Supremacy," in *Contemporary Issues in Political Philosophy*, eds. William R. Shea and John King-Farlow (New York: Science History Publications, 1976), 49–65.

52. Ruth Hubbard, "Have Only Men Evolved?," in *Women Look at Biology Looking at Women*, eds. Ruth Hubbard, Mary Sue Henifen, and Barbara Fried (Cambridge: Schenkman Publishing, 1979), 7–36.

53. Elaine Showalter, "Toward a Feminist Poetics," in *Essays on Women, Literature & Theory*, ed. Elaine Showalter (New York: Pantheon, 1985), 139.

54. Jane P. Tompkins, "Sentimental Power: *Uncle Tom's Cabin* and the Politics of Literary History," in *Essays on Women, Literature & Theory*, ed. Elaine Showalter (New York: Pantheon, 1995), 84.

55. Nancy Schrom Dye, "Clio's American Daughters: Male History, Female Reality," in *Prism of Sex*, eds. Julia A. Sherman and Evelyn Torton Beck (Madison: University of Wisconsin Press, 1979), 9–32.

56. Jane Roland Martin, *Changing the Educational Landscape* (New York: Routledge, 1994), Chap. 1.

57. Ibid., Chap. 12.

58. See, for example, Florence Howe, *Myths of Coeducation* (Bloomington: University of Indiana Press, 1984), 278.

59. Gloria Bowles and Renate Duelli Klein, "Introduction," in *Theories of Women's Studies*, eds. Gloria Bowles and Renate Duelli Klein (London: Routledge and Kegan Paul, 1983), 7.

60. "Women on the Faculty," 13.

61. Daphne Patai and Noretta Koertge, *Professing Feminism* (New York: Basic Books, 1994).

62. Mona Harrington, *Women Lawyers* (New York: Penguin, 1995), 67.

63. Meg Lovejoy, "'You Can't Go Home Again': The Impact of Women's Studies on Intellectual and Personal Development," *National Women's Studies Association Journal* 10 (1998): 127.

64. Ibid., 129.

65. Virginia Woolf, *A Room of One's Own* (New York: Harcourt Brace, 1929), 78.

66. Koldony, 3–4.

67. Gaard, 130.

68. Dale Bauer with Katharine Rhoades, "The Meanings and Metaphors of Student Resistance," in *Anti-Feminism in the Academy*, eds. VèVè Clark, Shirley Nelson Garner, Margaret Higonnet, and Ketu H. Katrak (New York: Routledge, 1996), 96.

69. Koldony, 8.

70. Susan Faludi, *Backlash* (New York: Doubleday, 1991), xxii.

71. Virginia Woolf, *Three Guineas* (New York: Harcourt Brace, 1938), 80.

72. Faludi, 278–9.
73. Ibid., 280.
74. Jane Roland Martin, *The Schoolhome* (Cambridge: Harvard University Press, 1992).
75. Bauer with Rhoades, 104.
76. Ibid., 105.
77. Gaard, 130.
78. Faludi, xxii.
79. Patai and Koertge, 214.
80. Ibid., xviii.
81. Mary Field Belenky, Blythe McVicker Clinchy, Nancy Rule Goldberger, and Jill Mattuck Tarule, *Women's Ways of Knowing* (New York: Basic Books, 1986).
82. Frances A. Maher and Mary Kay Thompson Tetreault, *The Feminist Classroom* (New York: Basic Books, 1994).
83. Dorothy C. Holland and Margaret A. Eisenhart, *Educated in Romance* (Chicago: University of Chicago Press, 1990).

IV. Assimilation or Transformation, That Is the Question

1. Oscar Handlin, *The Uprooted* (Boston: Little Brown, 1951), 262.
2. Theodore Caplow and Reece J. McGee, *The Academic Marketplace* (New York, Basic Books, 1958), 226.
3. Jill Ker Conway, *The Road from Coorain* (New York: Alfred A. Knopf, 1990), 171.
4. Ralph Beals, "Acculturation," in *Anthropology Today*, ed. A.L. Kroeber (Chicago: University of Chicago Press, 1953), 628.
5. Milton M. Gordon, *Assimilation in American Life* (New York: Oxford University Press, 1964), Chap. #4.
6. Dorothy C. Holland and Margaret A. Eisenhart, *Educated in Romance* (Chicago: University of Chicago Press, 1990), 104.
7. Ibid., 98.
8. Ibid.
9. John Stuart Mill, *The Subjection of Women* (Cambridge: The M.I.T. Press, 1970), 29.
10. Holland and Eisenhart, 104.

Part Three: Add Women and Transform

I. The Brain Drain

1. George Bernard Shaw, *Pygmalion* (New York: New American Library, 1975), 87.
2. Ibid., 80.
3. Willy Russell, *Educating Rita* (Harlow: Longman, 1985), 33.
4. Ibid., 18.
5. Ibid., 47–8.
6. Ibid., 62.
7. Richard Rodriguez, *Hunger of Memory* (Boston: David Godine, 1982), 70–71.
8. Ibid., 47.

9. Martha Nussbaum, *Cultivating Humanity* (Cambridge: Harvard University Press, 1997), 10.
10. Ibid., 191.
11. Ibid., 188.
12. Martha Nussbaum, "Women's Lot," *New York Review of Books*, 30 January 1986: 7–12.
13. Nussbaum, 1997, 9.
14. Ibid., 8.

II. TALES OF CONTAINMENT

1. Simone de Beauvoir, *The Second Sex* (New York: Bantam Books, 1961), xiii.
2. Ibid., xiv.
3. Ibid.
4. See, for example, Marilyn R. Schuster and Susan R. Van Dyne, "Curricular Change for the Twenty-first Century: Why Women?," in *Women's Place in the Academy*, eds. Marilyn R. Schuster and Susan R. Van Dyne (Totowa, N.J.: Littlefield & Allanheld, 1985), 19.
5. Pauli Murray, "The Liberation of Black Women," in *Voices of the New Feminism*, ed. Mary Lou Thompson (Boston: Beacon Press, 1970), 90.
6. Elsa Walsh, *Divided Lives* (New York: Doubleday, 1995).
7. Letty Cottin Pogrebin, "Competing with Women," in *Competition*, eds. Valerie Miner and Helen E. Longino (New York: Feminist Press, 1987), 13.
8. Ibid.
9. Ibid.
10. Ibid.
11. Mary Antin, *The Promised Land* (New York: Penguin Books, 1997), 144.
12. Randolph Bourne, "Trans-National America," in *Theories of Ethnicity*, ed. Werner Sollors (New York: New York University Press, 1996), 94.
13. Milton M. Gordon, *Assimilation in American Life* (New York: Oxford University Press, 1964), 71.
14. Ibid., 78.
15. Nathan Glazer, *We Are All Multiculturalists Now* (Cambridge: Harvard University Press, 1997),
16. Martha Nussbaum, *Cultivating Humanity* (Cambridge: Harvard University Press, 1987), 188.
17. Philip L. Quinn and Charles Taliaferro, eds., *A Companion to Philosophy of Religion* (Cambridge: Blackwell, 1997).
18. Robert Godin and Philip Pettit, eds. *Contemporary Political Philosophy* (Oxford: Blackwell, 1997).
19. C. Wennerås and A. Wold, "Nepotism and Sexism in Peer Review," *Nature* 387 (1997): 341–43.

III. ACTIONS GREAT AND SMALL

1. See, for example, Horace M. Kallen, *Culture and Democracy in the United States* (New York: Arno Press, 1970).
2. Milton M. Gordon, *Assimilation in American Life* (New York: Oxford University Press, 1964), 254ff.

Notes

3. Mary Field Belenky, Lynne A. Bond, and Jacqueline S. Weinstock, *A Tradition That Has No Name* (New York: Basic Books, 1997), 72.
4. Ibid., 4.
5. Ibid., 7.
6. Ibid.
7. Ibid., 58.
8. Ibid.
9. Ibid., 124.
10. Sandra Bartky, *Feminity and Domination* (New York: Routledge, 1990), 16.
11. Aristophanes, "Lysistrata," *Aristophanes Four Comedies*, ed. William Arrowsmith (Ann Arbor: Ann Arbor Paperbacks, 1969), 10ff, emphasis in the text.
12. Belenky et al., 7.
13. William Dray, *Laws and Explanation in History* (Oxford: Oxford University Press, 1957), Chap. VI.
14. "Insults and Injury: A Conversation with Heidi Weissmann," *The Women's Review of Books* XII (February 1996): 22.
15. Ibid., 23.
16. Ibid., 22.
17. Peter Applebome, "Can Harvard's Powerhouse Alter the Course of Black Studies?," *New York Times*, 3 November 1996, *Education Life*: 24.
18. Ibid., 27.
19. Ibid.
20. Patricia S. Mann, *Micro-Politics: Agency in a Postfeminist Era* (Minneapolis: University of Minnesota Press, 1994), 2.
21. Ibid., 4.
22. Ibid., 6.
23. bell hooks, *Feminist Theory: From Margin to Center* (Boston: South End Press, 1984), preface.
24. Ibid.

CONCLUSION

1. Susan J. Leonardi, *Dangerous by Degrees* (New Brunswick: Rutgers University Press, 1989).
2. Sandra Harding, "Feminism: Reform or Revolution," in *Women and Philosophy*, eds. Carol C. Gould and Marx W. Wartofsky (New York: Puntam's Sons, 1976), 271–84.
3. Jana Sawicki, "Foucault and Feminism: Toward a Politics of Difference," in *Feminist Interpretations and Political Theory*, eds. Mary Lydon Shanley and Carole Pateman (University Park: Penn State University Press, 1991), 223.
4. Ibid.

WORKS CITED

Addelson, Kathryn Pyne. "Comment on Ringelheim's 'Women and the Holocaust': A Reconsideration of Research." *Signs* 12 (1987): 830–33.

———. "Feminist Philosophy and the Women's Movement." *Hypatia* 9 (1994): 216–24.

Aisenberg, Nadya and Harrington, Mona. *Women of Academe.* Amherst: University of Massachusetts Press, 1988.

Alcoff, Linda. "Cultural Feminism versus Post-Structuralism: The Identity Crisis in Feminist Theory." *Signs* 13 (1988): 405–36.

Antin, Mary. *The Promised Land.* New York: Penguin Books, 1997.

Anzaldúa, Gloria, ed. *Making Face, Making Soul.* San Francisco: aunt lute books, 1990.

Applebome, Peter. "Can Harvard's Powerhouse Alter the Course of Black Studies?" *New York Times*, 3 Nov., *Education Life*: 24–28.

Aristophanes, "Lysistrata." Ed. William Arrowsmith. *Aristophanes Four Comedies.* Ann Arbor: Ann Arbor Paperbacks, 1969.

Backhouse, Constance, Roma Harris, Gillian Michell, and Alison Wylie. *The Chilly Climate for Faculty Women at UWO: Postscript to the Backhouse Report.* London, Ontario: University of Western Ontario, 1989.

Bartky, Sandra. *Femininity and Domination.* New York: Routledge, 1990.

Bauer, Dale with Katharine Rhoades. "The Meanings and Metaphors of Student Resistance." *Anti-Feminism in the Academy.* Eds. VèVè Clark, Shirley Nelson Garner, Margaret Higonnet, and Ketu H. Katrak. New York: Routledge, 1996: 95–114.

Beals, Ralph. "Acculturation." *Anthropology Today.* Ed. A L. Kroeber. Chicago: University of Chicago Press, 1953.

Belenky, Mary Field, Lynne A. Bond and Jacqueline S. Weinstock. *A Tradition That Has No Name.* New York: Basic Books, 1997.

Belenky, Mary Field, Blythe McVicker Clinchy, Nancy Rule Goldberger, and Jill Mattuck Tarule. *Women's Ways of Knowing.* New York: Basic Books, 1986.

Benckert, Sylvia, and Else-Marie Staberg. "Is It Really Worthwhile? Women Chemists and Physicists in Sweden." *Education into the 21st Century.* Eds. Alison Mackinnon, Inga Elgqvist-Saltzman, and Alison Prentice. London: Falmer Press, 1998. 118–30.

Berry, Wendell. *Standing by Words.* San Francisco: North Point Press, 1983.

Bogstad, Inga, and Elin Svenneby. "Gender—an Issue for Philosophy?" Oslo: Second Nordic Symposium of Women in Philosophy, 1994.

Bordo, Susan. "Feminism, Postmodernism, and Gender-Skepticism." *Feminism/Postmodernism.* Ed. Linda J. Nicholson. New York: Routledge, 1990. 133–56.

Bourne, Randolph. "Trans-National America." *Theories of Ethnicity.* Ed. Werner Sollors. New York: New York University Press, 1996. 93–108.

Bowles, Gloria. "Is Women's Studies an Academic Discipline?" *Theories of Women's Studies.* Eds. Gloria Bowles and Renate Duelli Klein. London: Routledge and Kegan Paul, 1983. 32–45.

Bowles, Gloria, and Renate Duelli Klein. "Introduction." *Theories of Women's Studies.* Eds. Gloria Bowles and Renate Duelli Klein. London: Routledge and Kegan Paul, 1983. 1–126.

Brown, Lyn Mike, and Carol Gilligan. *Meeting at the Crossroads.* Cambridge: Harvard University Press, 1992.

Brownmiller, Susan. *Femininity.* New York: Ballantine, 1984.

Bunch, Charlotte. "Not by Degrees: Feminist Theory and Education." *Quest* 5 (1979): 248–60.

Caplow, Theodore, and Reece J. McGee. *The Academic Marketplace.* New York: Basic Books, 1958.

Carpenter, Mary Wilson. "Female Grotesques in Academia." *Anti-Feminism in the Academy.* Eds. VèVè Clark, Shirley Nelson Garner, Margaret Higonnet, and Ketu H. Katrak. New York: Routledge, 1996. 141–65.

Carton, Barbara. "A Rebel in the Sisterhood." *Boston Globe,* 16 June 1994: 69, 74.

Chamberlain, Miriam K., ed. *Women in Academe.* New York: Russell Sage Foundation, 1988.

Chambers, Victoria. *Mama's Girl.* New York: Riverhead Books, 1996.

Chisholm, Shirley. "Women Must Rebel." *Voices of the New Feminism.* Ed. Mary Lou Thompson. Boston: Beacon Press, 1970. 207–16.

Chodorow, Nancy. *The Reproduction of Mothering.* Berkeley: University of California Press, 1978.

Clark, Lorenne. "The Rights of Women: The Theory and Practice of the Ideology of Male Supremacy." *Contemporary Issues in Political Philosophy.* Eds. William R. Shea and John King-Farlow. New York: Science History Publications, 1976. 49–65.

Clark, Margaret. *The Great Divide.* Canberra: Curriculum Development Centre, 1989.

Cohn, Carol. "Sex and Death in the Rational World of Defense Intellectuals." *Signs* 12 (1987): 687–718.

Conway, Jill Ker. *The Road from Coorain.* New York: Alfred A. Knopf, 1990.

Cullen, Kevin. "Breaking Thin Blue Line of Bias." *Boston Globe.* 16 Jan. 1996: 15–20.

de Beauvoir, Simone. *The Second Sex.* New York: Bantam Books, 1961.

de Lauretis, Teresa. "Upping the Anti [sic] in Feminist Theory." *Conflicts in Femi-*

nism. Eds. Marianne Hirsch and Evelyn Fox Keller. New York: Routledge, 1990. 255–70.

Diamond, Irene, and Lee Quinby, eds. *Feminism & Foucault.* Boston: Northeastern University, 1988.

Disch, Lisa, and Mary Jo Kane. "When a Looker Is Really a Bitch: Lisa Olson, Sport, and the Heterosexual Matrix." *Signs* 21 (1996): 278–308.

Doctoral Recipients from United States Universities. Washington D.C.: National Research Council, 1987.

Dray, William. *Laws and Explanation in History.* Oxford: Oxford University Press, 1957.

duCille, Ann. "The Occult of True Black Womanhood: Critical Demeanor and Black Feminist Studies." *Signs* 19 (1994): 591–629.

Dye, Nancy Schrom. "Clio's American Daughters: Male History, Female Reality." *The Prism of Sex.* Eds. Julia A. Sherman and Evelyn Torton Beck. Madison: University of Wisconsin Press, 1979: 9–32.

Echols, Alice. "The New Feminism of Yin and Yang." *Powers of Desire.* Eds. Ann Snitow, Christine Stansell, and Sharon Thompson. New York: Monthly Review Press, 1983. 439–59.

———. "The Taming of the Id: Feminist Sexual Politics, 1968–83." *Pleasure and Danger.* Ed. Carole S. Vance. Boston: Routledge and Kegan Paul, 1984. 50–72.

Eisenstein, Hester. *Contemporary Feminist Thought.* Boston: G. K. Hall, 1983.

Elbow, Peter. *Writing without Teachers.* New York: Oxford University Press, 1973.

Eliot, George. *Daniel Deronda.* 1876. London: Penguin Books, 1986.

Faludi, Susan. *Backlash.* New York: Doubleday, 1991.

Farley, Jennie. "Women Professors in the USA: Where Are They?" *Storming the Tower.* Eds. Suzanne Lie and Virginia O'Leary. London: Kogan Page, 1990. 194–207.

Fraser, Nancy, and Linda J. Nicholson. "Social Criticism without Philosophy: An Encounter between Feminism and Postmodernism." *Feminism/Postmodernism.* Ed. Linda J. Nicholson. New York: Routledge, 1990.

Gaard, Greta. "Anti-Lesbian Intellectual Harassment in the Academy." *Anti-Feminism in the Academy.* Eds. VèVè Clark, Shirley Nelson Garner, Margaret Higonnet, and Ketu H. Katrak. New York: Routledge, 1996. 115–40.

Gallop, Jane, Marianne Hirsch, and Nancy Miller. "Criticizing Feminist Criticism." *Conflicts in Feminism.* Eds. Marianne Hirsch and Evelyn Fox Keller. New York: Routledge, 1990. 349–69.

Gilligan, Carol. *In a Different Voice.* Cambridge: Harvard University Press, 1982.

———. "Joining the Resistance." *Michigan Quarterly Review* XXIX (1990): 501–36.

———. "Hearing the Difference: Theorizing Connection." *Hypatia* 10 (1995): 120–27.

———. "The Centrality of Relationship in Human Development: A Puzzle, Some Evidence, and a Theory." *Development and Vulnerability in Close Relationships.* Eds. Gil Noam and Kurt Fisher. New York: Lawrence Erlbaum, 1996. 237–61.

Gilligan, Carol, Janie Victoria Ward, and Jill McLean Taylor, eds. *Mapping the Moral Domain.* Cambridge: Harvard University Press, 1988.

Gilligan, Carol, Nona P. Lyons, and Trudy J. Hanmer, eds. *Making Connections.* Cambridge: Harvard University Press, 1990.

Works Cited

Glazer, Nathan. *We Are All Multiculturalists Now.* Cambridge: Harvard University Press, 1997.

Goodin, Robert E., and Philip Pettit, eds. *Contemporary Political Philosophy.* Oxford: Blackwell, 1997.

Goodman, Ellen. "Sexual Bullies." *Boston Globe.* 6 June 1993.

Gordon, Milton M. *Assimilation in American Life.* New York: Oxford University Press, 1964.

Greenblatt, Stephen, and Giles Gunn. "Introduction." *Redrawing the Boundaries.* Eds. Greenblatt and Gunn. New York: Modern Language Association of America, 1992. 1–11.

Gulbrandsen, Elisabeth. "Objectivity? Reflexivity! Authority?!" *Conditions of Our Knowing.* Eds. Åsa Andersson and Hildur Kalman. Umeå, Sweden: Nordic Network for Postgraduate Students in Feminist Epistemology and Feminist Philosophy of Science, 1995. 78–92.

Hall, Roberta M., and Bernice Resnick Sandler. *The Classroom Climate: A Chilly One for Women.* Washington D.C.: Association of Women's Colleges, 1982.

Handlin, Oscar. *The Uprooted.* Boston: Little Brown, 1951.

Harding, Sandra. "Feminism: Reform or Revolution." *Women and Philosophy.* Eds. Carol C. Gould and Marx W. Wartofsky. New York: G. P. Putnam's Sons, 1976. 271–84.

———. *The Science Question in Feminism.* Ithaca: Cornell University Press, 1986.

Harrington, Mona. *Women Lawyers.* New York: Penguin, 1995.

Holland, Dorothy C., and Margaret A. Eisenhart. *Educated in Romance.* Chicago: University of Chicago Press, 1990.

hooks, bell. *Ain't I a Woman.* Boston: South End Press, 1981.

———. *Feminist Theory: from margin to center.* Boston: South End Press, 1984.

———. *Talking Back.* Boston: South End Press, 1989.

Howe, Florence. *Myths of Coeducation.* Bloomington: University of Indiana Press, 1984.

Hubbard, Ruth. "Have Only Men Evolved?" *Women Look at Biology Looking at Women.* Eds. Ruth Hubbard, Mary Sue Henifin, Barbara Fried. Cambridge: Schenkman Publishing, 1979. 7–36.

Illich, Ivan. *Deschooling Society.* New York: Harper & Row, 1972.

"Insults and Injury: A Conversation with Heidi Weissmann." *Women's Review of Books.* February 1996. 21–23.

Jenkins, Richard. *Pierre Bourdieu.* London: Routledge, 1992.

Joeres, Ruth-Ellen Boetcher. "On Writing Feminist Academic Prose." *Signs* 17 (1992): 701–04.

Kallen, Horace M. *Culture and Democracy in the United States.* 1924. New York: Arno Press, 1970.

Keller, Evelyn Fox. *A Feeling for the Organism.* San Francisco: W. H. Freeman, 1983.

Kerber, Linda. "Some Cautionary Words for Historians." *Signs* 11 (1986): 304–10.

Koldony, Annette. "Paying the Price of Antifeminist Intellectual Harassment." *Anti-Feminism in the Academy.* Eds. VèVè Clark, Hairley Nelson Garner, Margaret Higonnet, and Ketu H. Katrak. New York: Routledge, 1996. 3–34.

Laird, Holly A. "Editing Feminist Journals: Report on the October 1993 Conference, 'Publishing Feminist Scholarship.'" *Chain* 1 (Summer 1994).

Lâm, Maivân Clech. "Feeling Foreign in Feminism." *Signs* 19 (1994): 865–93.

Lehigh, Scot. "Universities Flunk Idea Test." *Boston Globe.* 3 Mar. 1996: 69.

Leonardi, Susan J. *Dangerous by Degrees.* New Brunswick: Rutgers University Press, 1989.

Lerna, Gerda. "Placing Women in History." *Liberating Women's History.* Ed. Berenice A. Carroll. Urbana: University of Illinois Press, 1976. 357–68.

Lie, Suzanne Stiver, and Virginia O'Leary, eds. *Storming the Tower.* London: Kogan Page, 1990.

Lifton, Robert J. "In a Dark Time." *The Final Epidemic.* Eds. Ruth Adams and Susan Cullen. Chicago: Educational Foundation for Nuclear Science, 1981. 1–2.

Lorde, Audre. *Sister Outsider.* Trumansberg, New York: The Crossing Press, 1984.

Lovejoy, Meg. " 'You Can't Go Home Again': The Impact of Women's Studies on Intellectual and Personal Development." *National Women's Studies Association Journal* 10 (1998): 119–38.

Lugones, Maria. "Playfulness, 'World'-Travelling, and Loving Perception." *Making Face, Making Soul.* Ed. Gloria Anzaldúa. San Francisco: aunt lute books, 1990. 390–402.

———. "On the Logic of Pluralist Feminism." *Feminist Ethics.* Ed. Claudia Card. Lawrence, Kansas: University Press of Kansas, 1991. 35–44.

Maher, Frances A., and Mary Kay Thompson Tetreault. *The Feminist Classroom.* New York: Basic Books, 1994.

Mann, Patricia S. *Micro-Politics: Agency in a Postfeminist Era.* Minneapolis: University of Minnesota Press, 1994.

Martin, Biddy. "Feminism, Criticism, and Foucault." *Feminism & Foucault.* Eds. Irene Diamond and Lee Quinby. Boston: Northeastern University, 1988.

Martin, Michael. "Pedagogical Arguments for Preferential Hiring and Tenuring of Women Teachers in the University." *Women and Philosophy.* Eds. Carol Gould and Marx Wartofsky. New York: G. P. Putnams Sons, 1976. 325–33.

Martin, Jane Roland. *Reclaiming a Conversation.* New Haven: Yale University Press, 1985.

———. *The Schoolhome.* Cambridge: Harvard University Press, 1992.

———. *Changing the Educational Landscape.* New York: Routledge, 1994.

———. "Methodological Essentialism, False Difference, and Other Dangerous Traps." *Signs* 19 (1994): 630–57.

———. "Aerial Distance, Esotericism, and Other Closely Related Traps." *Signs* 21 (1996): 584–614.

———. "Bound for the Promised Land: The Gendered Character of Higher Education." *Duke Journal of Gender Law & Policy* 4 (1997): 3–26.

McLarin, Kimberly. "Radcliffe Alumnae Get Tough with Harvard." *New York Times.* 7 Jan. 1996. 19, 39.

Mead, Margaret. *Coming of Age in Samoa.* New York: William Morrow, 1928.

Mill, John Stuart. *The Subjection of Women.* 1869. Cambridge: MIT Press, 1970.

Millet, Kate. *Sexual Politics.* New York: Ballantine, 1978.

Morgan, Robin. *Sisterhood Is Powerful.* New York: Vintage, 1970.

Muller Joann. "Crimson-faced." *Boston Globe.* 22 April 1998.

Munkhammar, Inger. *What Does Public Statistics on Education Tell?* Stockholm: Statistics Sweden, 1996.

Works Cited

Murray, Pauli. "The Liberation of Black Women." *Voices of the New Feminism*. Ed. Mary Lou Thompson. Boston: Beacon Press, 1970. 87–102.

Nicholson, Linda J. *Gender and History*. New York: Columbia University Press, 1986.

Nussbaum, Martha. "Women's Lot." *New York Review of Books*. 30 Jan. 1986. 7–12.

———. *Cultivating Humanity*. Cambridge: Harvard University Press, 1997.

Okin, Susan Moller. *Women in Western Political Thought*. Princeton: Princeton University Press, 1979.

Orenstein, Peggy. *SchoolGirls*. New York: Doubleday, 1994.

Patai, Daphne, and Noretta Koertge. *Professing Feminism*. New York: Basic Books, 1994.

Plato. *Republic*. Trans. Grube. Indianapolis: Hackett Publishing, 1974.

Pogrebin, Letty Cottin. "Competing with Women." *Competition*. Eds. Valerie Miner and Helen E. Longino. New York: Feminist Press, 1987. 11–17.

Quinn, Philip L., and Charles Taliaferro, eds. *A Companion to Philosophy of Religion*. Cambridge: Blackwell, 1997.

Reiter, Rayna R., ed. *Toward an Anthropology of Women*. New York: Monthly Review Press, 1975.

Reuters. "Women Testify on Lewd and Harassing Behavior on Wall Street." *Boston Globe*. 23 Jan. 1998. 23.

Rhodes, Richard. *The Making of the Atomic Bomb*. New York: Simon & Schuster, 1988.

Rich, Adrienne. "Toward a Woman-Centered University." *On Lies, Secrets, and Silence*. New York: W. W. Norton, 1979.

Rodriguez, Richard. *Hunger of Memory*. Boston: David R. Godine, 1982.

Rosaldo, Michelle Zimbalist, and Louise Lamphere, ed. *Woman, Culture & Society*. Stanford: Stanford University Press, 1974.

Rousseau, Jean-Jacques. *Emile*. 1762. Trans. Allan Bloom. New York: Basic Books, 1979.

Russell, Willy. *Educating Rita*. Harlow: Longman, 1985.

Sadker, Myra and David Sadker. *Failing at Fairness*. New York: Touchstone, 1995.

Sandler, Bernice Resnick, Lisa A. Silverberg, and Roberta M. Hall. *The Chilly Classroom Climate: A Guide to Improve the Education of Women*. Washington D.C.: National Association for Women in Education, 1996.

Sawicki, Jana. "Foucault and Feminism: Toward a Politics of Difference." *Feminist Interpretations and Political Theory*. Eds. Mary Lyndon Shanley and Carole Pateman. University Park: Penn State University Press, 1991.

Schaller, Susan. *A Man without Words*. New York: Summit, 1991.

Schuster, Marilyn R., and Susan R. Van Dyne. "Curricular Change for the Twenty-first Century: Why Women?" *Women's Place in the Academy*. Eds. Marilyn R. Schuster and Susan R. Van Dyne. Totowa, N.J.: Littlefield & Allanheld, 1985. 3–12.

Schweickart, Patrocino P. "Speech Is Silver, Silence Is Gold." *Knowledge, Difference, and Power*. Eds. Nancy Goldberger, Jill Tarule, Blythe Clinchy, and Mary Belenky. New York: Basic Books, 1996. 305–31.

Scott, Joan. *Gender and the Politics of History*. New York: Columbia University Press, 1988.

"Shared Power, Responsibility." National Report by the Government of Sweden for the Fourth World Conference on Women in Beijing, 1995.

Shaw, Geroge Bernard. *Pygmalion.* New York: New American Library, 1975.

Sherman, Julia, and Evelyn Torton Beck, ed. *The Prism of Sex.* Madison: University of Wisconsin Press, 1979.

Showalter, Elaine. "Toward a Feminist Poetics." *Essays on Women, Literature & Theory.* Ed. Elaine Showalter. New York: Pantheon, 1985. 125–43.

Snitow, Ann. "A Gender Diary." *Conflicts in Feminism.* Eds. Marianne Hirsch and Evelyn Fox Keller. New York: Routledge, 1990. 9–43.

Solomon, Barbara. *In the Company of Educated Women.* New Haven: Yale University Press, 1985.

Spivak, Gayatri Chakravorty. "In a Word: Interview." *difference.* 1 (1989): 128–29.

Spelman, Elizabeth. *Inessential Woman.* Boston: Beacon Press, 1988.

Spender, Dale. *Invisible Women.* London: Writers and Readers Publishing, 1982.

Staberg, Else-Marie. "Gender and Science in the Swedish Compulsory School." *Gender and Education.* 6 (1994): 35–45.

Stacey, Judith. "On Resistance, Ambivalence and Feminist Theory: A Response to Carol Gilligan." *Michigan Quarterly Review.* XXIX (1990): 537–46.

Stein, Nan, and Lisa Sjpostrom. *Flirting or Hurting?* Washington D.C.: National Education Association, 1994.

Teng, Jinhua Emma. "The Construction of the 'Traditional Chinese Woman' in the Western Academy: A Critical Review." *Signs* 22 (1996): 115–51.

Thomas, Kim. *Gender and Subject in Higher Education.* Buckingham: Open University Press, 1990.

Tommasini, Anthony. "Academy Strings Ensemble Even Better 'Live.'" *Boston Globe.* 8 Oct. 1988: 16.

Tompkins, Jane P. "Sentimental Power: *Uncle Tom's Cabin* and the Politics of Literary History." *Essays on Women, Literature & Theory.* Ed. Elaine Showalter. New York: Pantheon, 1995. 81–104.

Veblen, Thorstein. *The Higher Learning in America.* 1918. New Brunswick: Transaction Publishers, 1993.

Walsh, Elsa. *Divided Lives.* New York: Doubleday, 1995.

Weisstein, Naomi. "Psychology Constructs the Female." *Woman in Sexist Society.* Eds. Vivian Gornick and Barbara K. Moran. New York: Basic Books, 1971. 133–46.

Wennerås, C., and A. Wold. "Nepotism and Sexism in Peer Review." *Nature* 387 (1997): 341–43.

West, Martha. "History Lessons." *Women's Review of Books.* February, 1996: 19–21.

Williams, Patricia. "Talking about Race, Talking about Gender, Talking about How We Talk." *Anti-Feminism in the Academy.* Eds. VèVè Clark, Shirley Nelson Garner, Margaret Higonnet, and Ketu H. Katrak. New York: Routledge, 1996. 69–94.

Wittgenstein, Ludwig. *Philosophical Investigations.* New York: Macmillan, 1953.

Wolf, Naomi. *Fire with Fire.* New York: Ballantine Books, 1993.

"Women Account for Half of College Enrollment in U.S., Three Other Nations." *Chronicle of Higher Education.* 17 Sept. 1986.

"Women on the Faculty." *Radcliffe Quarterly.* Fall/Winter, 1995: 10–16.

Works Cited

Woolf, Virginia. *A Room of One's Own*. New York: Harcourt Brace, 1929.

———. "Mary Wollstonecraft." *A Vindication of the Rights of Woman*. Ed. Carol H. Poston. New York: W. W. Norton, 1975.

———. *Three Guineas*. New York: Harcourt Brace Jovanovich, 1938.

Young, Michael. "Socially Organized Knowledge." *Knowledge and Control*. Ed. Michael F. D. Young. London: Collier Macmillan, 1971. 19–46.

INDEX

Index

Index